Palgrave Studies in Economic History

Series Editor
Kent Deng, London School of Economics, London, UK

Palgrave Studies in Economic History is designed to illuminate and enrich our understanding of economies and economic phenomena of the past. The series covers a vast range of topics including financial history, labour history, development economics, commercialisation, urbanisation, industrialisation, modernisation, globalisation, and changes in world economic orders.

Penelope Francks

Housework, Consumption and Female Labour in Japan, 1600–1940

Understanding the Role of Unpaid Work in Determining Living Standards

Penelope Francks
East Asian Studies
University of Leeds
Leeds, UK

ISSN 2662-6497   ISSN 2662-6500   (electronic)
Palgrave Studies in Economic History
ISBN 978-3-031-83692-3   ISBN 978-3-031-83693-0   (eBook)
https://doi.org/10.1007/978-3-031-83693-0

Cover illustration: © Harvey Loake

This Palgrave Macmillan imprint is published by the registered company Springer Nature
Switzerland AG
The registered company address is: Gewerbestrasse 11, 6330 Cham, Switzerland

If disposing of this product, please recycle the paper.

PREFACE

For practical reasons (the pandemic, my ageing eyesight, etc.) this work does not make extensive use of direct sources in Japanese, being more concerned to locate the Japanese case within the wider literature to which I argue it is importantly relevant. Most of the references are therefore to English-language material in economic history, feminist economics and Japanese studies which will be accessible to the broader readership at which the book is aimed. Nonetheless, it is ultimately based on a substantial body of research, by Japanese and Western-language scholars, into the history of everyday life and living standards in Japan, references to which can be found in, for instance, Susan Hanley's *Everyday Things in Premodern Japan* (Berkeley: University of California Press. 1997) or my own books and articles, as well as the footnotes that follow.

This book has been a solitary effort, eked out during the months of the pandemic and since, and I would simply like to thank my husband for keeping us safe and maintaining the supply of coffee. Thanks also to Ellie Duncan at Palgrave for her efficiency and support and to two enthusiastic readers who helped me believe I could do it one more time.

Leeds, UK   Penelope Francks

CONTENTS

LIST OF TABLES

CHAPTER 1

Introduction

Abstract This chapter introduces the main issues with which the book deals. It begins with the question of the definition of work and the ways in which standard assumptions have led to the absence of unpaid household labour, typically carried out by women, in the analysis and quantification of output and living standards in the past. Neglect of the contribution of unpaid labour poses particular problems for long-term and comparative studies and feminist scholars are beginning to research ingenious new data with which to overcome it. This study will consider the case of Japan, making use of analysis of the characteristics of Japanese consumer goods—principally food and clothing—as a means to assessing how unpaid and largely female labour contributed to the household's productive activities. It thereby introduces the idea that Japan may have followed a distinctly 'housework-intensive' path of development with significant implications for global comparisons.

Keywords Housework · Japanese economic development · Measurement of living standards · Japanese consumer goods

This short study examines two crucial aspects of our everyday lives—work and living standards—and the ways in which they have changed

© The Author(s), under exclusive license to Springer Nature Switzerland AG 2025
P. Francks, *Housework, Consumption and Female Labour in Japan, 1600–1940*, Palgrave Studies in Economic History,
https://doi.org/10.1007/978-3-031-83693-0_1

and interrelated over the course of economic development and industri-alisation in different historical contexts. It reflects, on the one hand, the large-scale research of recent years into the measurement and compar-ative assessment of living standards in the past and, on the other, the ways in which the emergence of 'feminist economics' is changing under-standing of the nature of work and the role of women within it. The link between the two is provided by the concept of 'housework'—the unpaid labour which is essential to the maintenance and improvement of living standards but necessarily unrecognised in the quantitative assessments on which historical analysis has largely been based.

Central to the issues with which this book is concerned, therefore, is the question of what should count as 'work' or, in economist's terms, labour input into the production of output.[1] Since the Industrial Revo-lution and the emergence of the factory, it has come to be assumed that work is the activity at which economically active individuals labour for wage, salary or profit, typically away from home and for an outside employer. The income earned is then used to acquire the goods and services the worker needs to survive and hopefully prosper. The value of work can be measured in terms of the wages and salaries earned by the paid labour force, as recorded in the kinds of official data sources that are likely to have survived from the past. Other forms of work appear 'unpaid' since they do not result in a wage paid to an individual, even if they entitle the worker to a share in the overall income of the household or other work-group.

Since the 1980s, however, there has emerged a growing recognition that a significant proportion of the 'work' that is necessary to make our everyday lives comfortable, secure and enjoyable does not necessarily take this form. In fact, much of the time not spent 'at work' has to be devoted to a wide range of activities that make the consumption of goods possible. Gary Becker famously pioneered what has come to be called the 'new household economics' on the basis of the assumption that the welfare of the household depends on more than just the purchases of goods in the market that its wages support.[2] Bought food cannot be consumed before at least some efforts at preparation; few of the other goods we buy

---

[1] For a more detailed discussion of the issues involved in defining work, see Sarti et al. (2018).

[2] Becker (1965). For a summary, see Tanimoto (2012: 27–28).

can be put to use without time spent absorbing them into consumption habits. As a result, even in the modern market economy, household labour makes an 'invisible' contribution to living standards and welfare and the household has to decide on the allocation of its time between the paid work that makes possible the purchase of goods in the market and the unpaid 'housework' that enables and supports their consumption.

In this context, the emergence of 'feminist economics' has resulted in growing demand for the recognition of housework as a form of 'work'.[3] In the political sphere, Italian MPs have pressed for the introduction of a 'housewife's wage' (Gissi, 2018); academic researchers have sought out ingenious forms of evidence as to how women in the past distributed their time between work inside and outside the home and made contributions to living standards that are invisible in other kinds of source.[4] The economic value of housework activities is reflected in the fact that, even if more-or-less enjoyable to many, most can be performed for payment, by servants or nowadays by specialised services. However, although it is possible to purchase most of the services an individual or family needs to survive—the cleaning, washing, child-minding, budget management and so on—for a wage, most households do not fulfil anything like all their needs this way, either from choice or because they cannot afford the cost. The recent pandemic has only increased our recognition of the value of what 'unpaid' labour within the household can contribute to our lives. In contemporary life, even our furniture can require a considerable input of labour on the part of the consumer if it is to be assembled, the economic value of which is demonstrated in the emergence of businesses that can be paid to perform the service.

Historically, moreover, although the concept of 'housework' would probably not have been recognised by pre-industrial people, it is the case that the further back in time one goes, the greater the share of economic activity carried out 'unpaid' within the household is likely to have been. In pre-industrial societies, as in many parts of the developing world today, a large proportion of household consumption goods will have been supplied through subsistence activities that did not require much, if any, involvement with whatever markets existed. Output would have been

---

[3] For a bibliography of literature on efforts to take account of unpaid labour in national accounting, see Sarti et al. (2018: 13 and n10).

[4] See, e.g., the use of court records in Shepard (2015) or Whittle and Hailwood (2020).

pooled and shared and no records of wages or employment would have been kept by which to measure the labour input and resulting contribution of 'invisible' household workers. Does this matter? A growing literature is now coming to argue that it does for two main reasons.

The first involves the assessment and measurement of output levels, labour input and living standards in the past. This may seem like an arcane issue of concern only to quantitatively minded economic historians but, given the power of numbers, the tables and statistical series that can be produced from measurable data have an influence well beyond those aware of how they were calculated. Estimates of, for example, Gross Domestic Product (GDP) per capita in the past look like their present-day equivalents and have come to be used as indicators of living standards and general levels of development, just as they are in contemporary economies. But, as we shall see, to the extent that a much larger share of productive activity in the past is likely to fall below the radar of market-based quantitative records, the standard of living of past societies will be under-estimated. Hence, we will picture the world out of which modern development emerged as more primitive and poor than it was and subsequent growth will appear all the more spectacular. International comparisons will be biased towards societies in which quantifiable output and labour have the greater share, even if, elsewhere, the goods and services so measured continue to be supplied by 'unpaid' household activities.

The second concerns the role of women in the economy and it is indeed the emerging body of feminist economists who have led the way in analysing the effects of the neglect of unpaid household labour on our understanding of economic activity in the past. Although by no means all 'housework' is carried out by women, we know from experience that their share of it tends to be greater. Hence more of the work carried out by women is likely to fall into the unrecorded and unmeasured category and their contribution to output and living standards will be under-estimated. In the estimation of the inputs into overall output, women's contribution is generally assumed to be limited—an unchanging 30% of total labour input in Broadberry et al.'s estimates of GDP and its sources for Britain up to the mid-nineteenth century, for example—as a result of child-bearing and the demands of 'housework' restricting women's participation in the paid labour force.[5] As Chapter 2 will show, this assumption is now being challenged by a growing body of research into the nature and scale of women's productive activity in the past, whether formally paid or not, and whether performed within or outside the home.

Recognition of the role of housework, and unpaid household labour in general, in the determination of living standards, even today but more so in the past, poses particular problems for those engaged in long-term historical and comparative studies. The scope for unpaid household labour in any individual economy will be determined by the institutional structures of employment and the family and will change over time and differ across societies. Most of the growing literature on historical living standards, housework and women's contribution to development has been concerned with Britain and to some extent other parts of Europe.[6] This book uses a rather different example—that of Japan—to suggest a different angle on these issues. Japan was for long the only country outside Europe and North America to achieve industrialisation and, as Chapter 3 describes, did so on the basis of a distinctive institutional structure which preserved the small-scale farm and household-based business well into the industrial period. This suggests that the scope of household-based labour, for which individual wages were not paid, was likely to have been greater and more persistent than in other examples of industrialisation, with significant implications for comparative understanding of living standards and their evolution over time.

In addition, greater scope for unpaid household labour is likely to imply a significant role for women in supporting household welfare and living standards which cannot be reflected in quantitative data. The contribution of women to the growth that preceded and accompanied industrialisation is hard to assess for any country, in the absence of the kinds of time-use survey used nowadays to discover the nature of work and who performed it. Given this, for the Japanese case, I have turned to some novel forms of evidence, looking at the characteristics of consumption goods as a means to deduce how they must have been produced

---

[5] Broadberry et al. (2015: 352–355). For a critical examination of Broadberry et al.'s estimates, see Whittle (2019: 46–48).

[6] In addition to the many Italian examples in Sarti et al. (2018), related work on Spain, France, the Low Countries and Scandinavia is already quite substantial, as the citations in Chapter 2 will demonstrate.

and by whom. This leads to the conclusion that Japan followed a strikingly 'housework-intensive' path of development, with results still to be observed in the distinctive Japanese consumption goods that have now 'gone global'. So, next time you eat a meal of steamed rice or noodles, flavoured with miso or pickles, remember that, although nowadays probably produced in fields and factories far from Japan, it was the 'unpaid' labour and skills of Japanese households, their female members in particular, that created the original forms of the goods you, alongside millions across the globe, are now enjoying.

Finally, we return to the original 'what is work?' question, since any assessment of the role of unpaid household labour in production must depend on how it is defined. Whittle and Hailwood (2020: 8–9) use the so-called third party rule whereby 'any unpaid work that could be replaced with paid work or purchased goods should be considered as work' (see also Whittle, 2019: 57). This definition clearly covers housework, care-work and childcare, all of which could (and still can) be performed by servants or other hired workers, but also extends to unpaid contributions to work in farming, food processing and household-based manufacturing activities. This is helpful in the context of the present study, which focuses on the production of the household's consumer goods—principally food and clothing—as evidenced in their characteristics, but also presents a means of assessing the extent to which the whole range of unpaid household activities contributed to living standards. Different societies, at different stages in their development, have demonstrated different degrees of reliance on the market, as against their own unpaid household work, for the goods and services they require but this should not affect our assessments of labour contributions and the value of output.

References

Becker, A. (1965). A theory of the allocation of time. *Economic Journal, 75*(299), 493–517.

Broadberry, S., Campbell, B., Klein, A., Overton, M., & van Leeuwen, B. (2015). *British economic growth 1270–1870*. Cambridge University Press.

Gissi, A. (2018). The home as factory: Rethinking the debate on housewives' wages in Italy, 1929–1980. In R. Sarti, A. Bellavitis, & M. Martini (Eds.), *What is work? Gender at the crossroads of home, family, and business from the early modern era to the present* (pp. 27–60). Berghahn Books.

Sarti, R., Bellavitis, A., & Martini, M. (2018). *What is work? Gender at the crossroads of home, family, and business from the early modern era to the present.* Berghahn Books.

Shepard, A. (2015). Crediting women in the early modern English economy. *History Workshop Journal, 79*, 1–24.

Tanimoto, M. (2012). The role of housework in everyday life: Another aspect of consumption in modern Japan. In P. Francks & J. Hunter (Eds.), *The historical consumer: Consumption and everyday life in Japan, 1850–2000* (pp. 27–55). Palgrave Macmillan.

Whittle, J. (2019). A critique of approaches to 'domestic work': Women, work and the pre-industrial economy. *Past and Present, 243*, 35–70.

Whittle, J., & Hailwood, M. (2020). The gender division of labour in early modern England. *Economic History Review, 73*(1), 3–32.

CHAPTER 2

Housework and Living Standards in the Literature

Abstract The Great Divergence debate, resulting from Kenneth Pomeranz's work comparing pre-industrial levels of development in Europe and China, stimulated significant new research into the techniques for measuring and comparing standards of living over time and space. These techniques were derived from work on England and tended to assume that household incomes largely depended on the market wage of a male 'breadwinner'. However, more recent work by feminist economic historians has begun to show that women in fact performed a wide range of productive labour, paid and unpaid, in pre-industrial and industrialising European economies. Moreover, recognition of the continuing contribution of women's work, unpaid labour and subsistence production to household income can be shown to have a significant impact on the assessment of living standards and their comparison across time and space.

Keywords Great Divergence · Comparison of living standards · Breadwinner household · Women's work · Subsistence production

This chapter outlines the emergence of unpaid labour, and women's work in general, from longstanding neglect in the analysis of the process of economic development and industrialisation. I argue that this reflects, not

P. Francks, *Housework, Consumption and Female Labour in Japan, 1600–1940*, Palgrave Studies in Economic History, https://doi.org/10.1007/978-3-031-83693-0_2

just the rise of 'feminist economics', but also the new directions in global economic history that have resulted from the so-called Great Divergence debate on why the Industrial Revolution occurred when and where it did. This debate came to hinge on comparisons of historical living standards and the work and incomes of households that determined them. It built on concepts such as the 'industrious revolution' and the 'consumer revolution' that described the ways in which households came to work harder and differently, as they sought to take advantage of the expanding range of commercial consumption possibilities opened up by trade and technological developments. A growing body of research on how household economies operated in the early-modern and industrialising periods, principally in Europe, is now revealing the central role of women and their work, paid and unpaid, in this process and more widely in the developments that led up to and sustained the Industrial Revolution.

HOUSEHOLDS, WOMEN'S WORK AND THE GREAT DIVERGENCE

It had long been assumed, in academic and popular literature, that 'modern' economic growth, and the social and cultural transformations that it involved, took off as a result of the Industrial Revolution that began in late eighteenth-century Britain. It was also typically accepted that the revolution occurred when and where it did on the basis of preconditions determined by longstanding developments in northern Europe, whether economic, institutional, cultural or whatever, that created the stimulus required.[1] European 'superiority' over the rest of the world in the run-up to the Industrial Revolution was thus the key factor behind the technological inventions that opened up the potential of new sources of energy and the emergence of the institutional structures of capitalism that enabled them to be exploited. This was reflected in the apparently superior pre-industrial economic capacity and living standards of 'the West', as compared with the still poor and primitive 'East'.

The consensus behind this view was to be shattered in 2000 with the publication of Kenneth Pomeranz's groundbreaking study of what he called 'the Great Divergence' (Pomeranz, 2000). In it he argued, on

---

[1] For a succinct summary of approaches to explaining the Industrial Revolution, see Allen (2009: ch. 1).

the basis of crucial indicators such as GDP per capita as well as a range of more qualitative evidence, that by the eighteenth century the Yangtse Basin in China was as well placed as England and Holland in terms of the conditions for an industrial revolution. Evidence of consumption levels, the spread of commercial activities, technological capacities and much more was presented in support of the argument that nothing in the comparative levels of pre-industrial economic, social or institutional development could explain the emergence of the Industrial Revolution in Britain and not China.[2]

Pomeranz's evidence and the implications he drew from it were to be strongly contested. This led to much work on the measurement of living standards and to a new interest in the ways in which they were determined within households across the Divergence. Central to this was the work of the University of California economic historian Jan de Vries, whose concept of an 'industrious revolution' as a precondition for full-scale industrialisation in Europe proved an influential advance in understanding of how early-modern households adapted, in the face of a growing and commercialising economy.[3] De Vries presented evidence that, by the second half of the seventeenth century, households in Holland, in particular, appeared to be working longer hours and engaging more in wage labour so as to acquire the cash incomes needed to buy new consumer goods that were appearing on the market (de Vries, 2008: 40–58). Better furniture, decorations and household equipment were becoming essential elements in a 'respectable' lifestyle, while newly-available imported goods, such as tea, coffee and chocolate, opened up enjoyable consumption possibilities for those with cash to spend. By the eighteenth century, patterned cotton textiles from India were becoming essential fashion items in European cities, stimulating domestic producers to find ways to compete with cheap but attractive fabrics.

From the point of view of the Great Divergence, the crucial question focused on whether or not a pre-industrial industrious revolution could have occurred on the other side of the divide from the commercialising regions of northern Europe central to de Vries's work. De Vries himself

---

[2] For a more detailed summary of Pomeranz's argument and evidence, see Francks (2016: ch. 1).

[3] De Vries (2008). De Vries also takes his argument beyond the early-modern and Industrial Revolution periods, linking it to the emergence of the 'breadwinner household' from the later nineteenth century, as later described.

argued that, in the Japanese case at least, the spread of the market and the rate of commercialisation remained too low to enable the mechanisms of the model to operate. This has been challenged and it certainly seems to have been the case that labour input into agriculture and manufacturing was increasing from the late eighteenth century onwards.[4] As later chapters will suggest, the Japanese case might imply that it is not always market-acquired goods that provide the incentive to work harder, if the consumption pattern offers scope for increases and improvements in the household's own production of consumer goods.

At any rate, de Vries's work, and the Great Divergence debate in general, helped to shift the focus of attention in global and comparative history away from macro aggregates and towards the ways in which pre-industrial households interacted with markets and allocated their resources, in the face of expanding employment and consumption opportunities. This became inter-twined with the emergence of feminist economics, as economic historians of Europe began to recognise and analyse the role of women and their labour in the growth that led up to and accompanied the Industrial Revolution. Influential work focused on the ways in which, in parts of northern Europe, new employment opportunities in workshops and small factories drove productive activities, for men and women, out of the home and into the market. The resulting wage-based employment provided the sources of income that enabled young people to marry and establish their own households with less parental influence, once they had accumulated the necessary resources, thus establishing what has become known as the 'European marriage pattern' of late marriage and nuclear families.[5] The pattern meant that young women remained in the labour force for relatively long periods before marriage and significant numbers never married at all, resulting in what de Moor and van Zanden (2010) labelled 'girl power', as single women came to play more important roles in the labour market and commercial world.

Later marriage led to lower birth rates, as well as greater opportunity to build up women's labour-force skills and experience, giving rise

---

[4] See the debate between de Vries and Osamu Saitō in the *Australian Economic History Review.* Saitō (2010) and de Vries (2011).

[5] For a recent survey of the literature on the European Marriage Pattern, see Merouani and Perrin (2022: 625–626). For more detail, see de Moor and van Zanden (2010).

to the argument that the changing nature of marriage and the household must have been an element in Europe's more favourable conditions for industrialisation.[6] In fact, in many parts of Europe, especially in the south, household-based production supported by extended-family institutions persisted, but in the north living standards increasingly came to depend on the wages that men and women brought into their independent nuclear households. Hence, as the next section describes, market wage rates have been central to the measurement of both labour input and living standards in the Great Divergence debate and more widely.

Given this, the inherent difficulties involved in finding evidence of women's contribution to household income encouraged researchers to rely on more easily available evidence of male wage rates as the measure of living standards.[7] As described below women's income-earning activity has tended to be more sporadic than men's and harder to measure. Women's responsibilities for childcare and 'housework' have typically been assumed to take priority, with wage-work or household production activities fitted around them. However, in recent years historians have begun to question these assumptions and to devise new ways of assessing and even measuring the contribution of women's paid and unpaid household activities to overall output and living standards. In a striking example, You (2024) argues that accurate inclusion of the numbers of paid and unpaid female domestic servants in mid-nineteenth-century English censuses would raise their total to over a million, more than the entire labour force in manufacturing industry. Horrel et al. (2021: 93) conclude from their detailed analysis of the issue in relation to England that 'at no time until later industrialization in the six centuries studied could a respectable standard be attained through men's work alone'.

Nonetheless, as the next section goes on to consider, the difficulties involved in making an accurate assessment of women's contribution to household income have continued to result in an over-reliance on more easily available data on male wage rates to measure labour input and

---

[6] Pomeranz (2000: 40–41) disputes this, arguing that fertility control within marriage was widespread in pre-industrial East Asia, leading to similar results. Evidence from Japan will appear in the next chapter.

[7] For the reasons why women's contribution to household income tends to be underestimated in quantitative analysis of living standards, see, e.g., Humphries and Sarasúa (2012) or Burnette (2021).

living standards. As the subsequent section describes, the nature and scale of women's contribution is bound to reflect the range of forces that determine household organisation, the nature of women's work, and the wider economic scope for unpaid productive activity. There will clearly be cross-national differences in the ways in which these forces operate, meaning that methods and models based on, for example, England may not represent the most appropriate means of assessing the contribution of women and unpaid work to household output and income elsewhere.[8] Relative under/over-estimation of this contribution would be reflected in measures of the inputs and outputs of households and hence in assessments of relative living standards across regions or nations with different economic and institutional structures. Chapters 3 and 4 will attempt to illustrate this, using the Japanese example.

WAGES, LIVING STANDARDS AND THE BREADWINNER HOUSEHOLD

In the light of the Great Divergence debate, since the 1980s, economic historians have devoted huge efforts to the collection and analysis of quantitative data that would enable them to produce the national-level estimates of outputs and inputs on which to base assessments of long-term growth and global comparisons. From the point of view of the debate, the Holy Grail has been an acceptable set of estimates of GDP (total national output) per capita over a long period for the country or region concerned. Despite the many problems with the use of GDP as a measure of sustainable welfare, this was seen as the only indicator of general living standards that it was feasible to calculate and compare over time or across borders. The revisionist work carried out by Crafts and Harley in the 1980s pioneered the use of econometric techniques in estimating GDP and established the methodology for the now-accepted estimates of the

---

[8] In a recent article (Burnette 2024), Joyce Burnette argues that England is in fact an 'outlier', as regards the reliance of households on male wages as the source of their livelihoods. Her evidence suggests that European households in general, into the twentieth century, continued to derive a significant share of their income from a range of activities, including women's work and subsistence production, so that their living standards were measurably less dependent on male wages than those of their English counterparts.

growth of output per capita in England since pre-industrial times, against which all other comparisons are made.[9]

Quantitative historical data on which to base estimates of measurable output at the national level (e.g. yields of agriculture or production of manufactured goods) vary from place to place and reflect all kinds of regional differences, but can generally be aggregated, using local market prices, to give national totals, at least for benchmark years. However, going further than this requires measurement of the inputs that went into this output and hence the productivity of land, labour and capital that ultimately determines living standards. The crucial data concern labour input and its cost, but here major problems with the sources emerge. The data that is available, in records of wage rates, factory statistics and so on, almost invariably relate to male workers, so that historians have little option but to base their estimates of the female contribution to output on very rough assumptions. Much of this work has been concerned with estimating female 'participation rates', as measured by participation in wage labour, and the relatively low rates that emerged were taken to imply that women's contribution to the economic output measured by GDP was comparatively small.[10]

Underlying this, as various feminist scholars have pointed out, lie assumptions, on the part of officials, statisticians and data-collectors in general, as to the nature of female work and the role of women within the household labour force (Humphries and Sarasúa 2012: 44–50). Census-takers assumed that men had an occupation and earned a steady wage, whereas the possibly more variable and informal occupations of women were not recorded. Shepard's analysis of a large number of witness statements by women to courts in England during the sixteenth and seventeenth centuries reveals the wide range of productive activities in which female workers engaged, often making an indispensable contribution to household incomes, even if very few gave themselves an occupational title—not even 'labourer'—that census-takers could record (Shepard, 2015). The approach of historical officials has necessarily carried over to those who use the data they collected, so that estimates of labour input into national output essentially depend on records of men's

---

[9] For a short account of the methods of estimating historical GDP, see Broadberry et al. (2015: xxi—xxxix). For more detail on England, see Griffen (2010: ch. 2).

[10] E.g. Broadberry et al. (2015: 352–355).

work. This is justified on the grounds that women's continuing responsibility for childcare and housework restricted their participation in the paid labour market and made their contribution to overall output invisible and/or impossible to measure.

Thus the idea that the living standards of households depend on male incomes became embedded in quantitative analyses and comparisons. De Vries had already argued that, following the increased labour-force participation of men and women during the industrious-revolution phase in Europe, rising male wages resulting from the expansion of industrial employment enabled women to withdraw from the labour force, giving rise to the 'male breadwinner household' assumed to prevail in industrial societies (de Vries, 2008: ch. 5). This also reflected, it was argued, a shift in demand preferences away from goods and towards household services, as health, education and comfort became more highly valued through the nineteenth century. In the past, such services had frequently been supplied by servants and other paid workers, as they increasingly are now, but the strengthening ideology of the housewife's role reallocated them to the unpaid labour of female household members. While in the early-modern period, the concept of 'housewife/housework' as we now know it did not exist, the 'good housewife' of industrial times withdrew from the labour market (if her husband earned enough) and devoted herself to the unpaid work of providing and managing household services. These services, if unpaid, have not been included in measurements of GDP, even though most of them could have been purchased and did have a market value. Hence, famously, if a man marries his housekeeper, GDP falls (since the housekeeper was paid a measurable wage but the wife is not), even if the cooking still gets done and everyone has something to eat.

The concept of the male breadwinner household has therefore come to permeate the global comparisons of living standards that the Great Divergence debate initiated. Such comparisons faced considerable difficulties resulting from the need to convert local prices for goods to an international standard, but even if household incomes could be estimated in a comparable way, global variations in diets and consumption patterns in general made it difficult to know what to include in determining the cost of living and so estimating what those incomes could buy. Robert Allen has devised an ingenious solution to these problems that involves the use of whatever historical surveys are available to determine the value of a 'subsistence basket', supplying an adequate number of calories but reflecting local diets and consumption preferences, for any given region. Prevailing wage rates can then be expressed in terms of the number of subsistence baskets that they could purchase—the 'welfare ratio'—and this could be compared cross-nationally and cross-culturally as well as through time. Hence, while wage rates in, for example, China might appear very low when converted at prevailing exchange rates and compared with European ones, when measured in terms of the welfare ratio, the differences are nowhere near so great (Allen et al., 2011).

Of course the wage rates used to estimate welfare ratios were typically the male ones for which records survived, reinforcing the breadwinner model. The contributions of female household members, whether monetary or, even more problematically, unpaid, could not be reflected in conclusions and comparisons concerning living standards. Hence the relative contribution of women's work to the quantity and quality of goods and services available to household members remains largely invisible and cross-national comparisons of living standards cannot reflect differences in the scope of this contribution.

In recent years, it has come to be recognised that very similar problems exist in relation to assessments of the GDP and living standards of present-day developing countries, where unpaid female labour often appears to be essential to the survival and welfare of households, and new measures are being devised to try to reflect the contribution of unpaid labour to household income (Whittle, 2019: 36–37). This necessarily enhances the importance of female labour and offsets the neglect of women's contribution that traditional measures involve. However, the focus on measurement has tended to divert attention from historical research into what women actually did and why it varied over time and across societies. A growing body of recent research is now correcting this neglect and the next section summarises available evidence on this, mostly relating to Europe.

BREADWINNER WAGES AND HOUSEHOLD LABOUR IN INDUSTRIALISING EUROPE

The recognition of the potential significance of unpaid and female labour to output and living standards has emerged out of the growing body of work on how households operated during the early-modern period and subsequent industrialisation and on women's role within this.[11] Jane Humphries and Jane Whittle have led the way with detailed studies, based on records of household budgets, wages and other evidence, both quantitative and qualitative, from English regions. Interest has now spread to other parts of northern and southern Europe, such as Spain and Sweden.[12] The accumulating evidence from this work means that Broadberry et al.'s (2015: 352–355) assumption of a constant female contribution to overall output in England of 30%, constrained by the demands of housework and care-work, throughout the period from the thirteenth century to the mid-nineteenth looks far from the mark. However, perhaps the most important conclusion so far is still Horrell, Humphries and Weisdorf's (2021: 93) demonstration that English households over long periods of development could not have managed without women's contribution to income and welfare.

This contribution clearly took varied and flexible forms that are hard to measure. Although quantifiable evidence is very limited, even for England as the most examined case, it seems that from the early-modern period onwards women did widely work for wages or piece-rates, even if not on a permanent basis (e.g. Whittle & Hailwood, 2020). Female employees and family members played vital roles in the seasonal agricultural labour force in England, for instance. However, both before and during the Industrial Revolution, it was the textile industries that offered women the widest opportunities for remunerated employment. The household-based spinning and weaving that drove the growth of textile production in, for example, northern England was largely carried out by women, with whole households mobilising to support female textile workers within the home. Textile workshops, and eventually factories, employing women were springing up across Europe even before modern industrialisation began, but thereafter, women were to occupy a major share of the factory work-force as the Industrial Revolution took place.

---

[11] For a recent survey of the now-substantial literature on women's role in the development process, together with a comprehensive bibliography, see Merouani and Perrin (2022).

[12] See e.g. Carmen Sarasúa's work on Spain, such as Sarasúa (2019), which shows how recognition of the widespread but previously neglected participation of women in industrial work significantly changes understanding of the pattern of Spanish industrialisation, or Maria Ågren's highly innovative approach to the case of Sweden, involving analysis of linguistic terms used to describe work and those performing it (Ågren, 2018).

Nonetheless, few women across Europe relied on their own wage-work to provide adequate support for themselves and their children. Most continued to live in households—parental or marital—and to use wage-work where they could get it to supplement overall household income. In fact, ingenious sources of evidence reveal women working in a range of income-earning activities, often from home (see e.g. Whittle, 2014). Retailing and commerce were frequently organised and carried out by women; women typically managed household finances and involved themselves in financial activities such as pawnbroking; the provision of hospitality for travellers was often women's work. It was not until the late nineteenth century that such activities came to be organised on a larger scale using male management and employees, to be replaced as sources of female employment by domestic service, dress-making, shop work and eventually clerical work, as urbanisation and industrialisation proceeded.

At the same time, although many women throughout Europe worked for wages at least part of the time, it must have been the case that they combined this with the housework activities essential to the survival and comfort of the household. The evidence suggests that women continued to be largely responsible for childcare and the health of household members; the acquisition and preparation of food was of course typically a female responsibility. However, the gender division of labour among household members rarely seems to have been fixed, with men frequently contributing to 'housework' and women mobilised to take part in many areas of production, especially in agriculture, as required (e.g. Ågren, 2018).

Nonetheless, food preparation remained central to housework activities, reflecting the fact that, even in industrial societies, few of the inputs into consumption that come into the household can be consumed without substantial preparation, and agricultural/food historians provide many examples of the activities required to process and preserve, as well as cook, whatever the household acquired.[13] This is of course especially the case where subsistence production supplies a significant portion of household needs. In England, given the landownership system and the early spread of relatively large-scale commercial farming, the scope for subsistence production was declining, even before the acceleration in urbanisation caused by the Industrial Revolution. The enclosure of

---

[13] See for example much evidence on food preparation and preservation in England throughout Thirsk (2006).

common land from the sixteenth century onwards deprived rural households of communal grazing and foraging resources and left them reliant on no more than garden plots for any self-supplied food they consumed (Gazeley & Horrell, 2013: 762–765; Overton, 1996: 133–167).

Elsewhere in Europe, however, small-scale farming, combining commercial and subsistence activities, continued, while the share of home-grown produce in household food supply remained significantly higher than in England. Boter (2020) shows that, in the Netherlands as late as the early twentieth century, even households whose main source of income was manufacturing relied on self-supplied goods from their small plots of land to achieve their satisfactory lifestyles. Burnette's (2024) evidence shows that the living standards of households across mainland Europe continued to be enhanced by self-supplied goods, raising their total incomes to levels much closer to those of English households largely reliant on the male breadwinner's wages. Looking after the family's cow, pig or chickens was standard work for women and girls. Cultivation of fruit and vegetables for home consumption remained common, while hunting and foraging were regular activities, wherever woodland and forests were accessible. All these activities generated produce that had to be processed and preserved using household labour but resulted in a standard of living above what would otherwise have been possible.

However, by the time of the Industrial Revolution, in most parts of Europe, few rural, and even fewer urban households lived on their own subsistence production alone. Rather they combined it with wage-work or commercial activities, so as to generate a cash contribution to household income. Women thus provided the flexibility needed to take advantage of income-earning opportunities in fields such as textiles, fitting wage-work or self-employment around the demands of childcare, food preparation and household management in general. Their contribution may not have been stable and a significant share of it must have fallen into the unpaid category, but the evidence suggests that few households could have managed to provide an adequate standard of living without it.

As a result, we cannot assume that male wages alone represent an adequate basis for assessing comparative living standards across different economies, societies and cultures. The nature of the contribution made by unpaid and female labour certainly makes it very difficult to measure and compare, but neglect of its significance for the living standards of households in the past undermines the comparisons over time and across regions that have emerged from the Great Divergence debate. The following chapters will use the Japanese example to examine the issues involved from a different angle, looking at what might determine the scope of unpaid household labour in a particular context and how it might be observed in the pattern of consumption over time.

REFERENCES

Ågren, M. (2018). The complexities of work: Analyzing men's and women's work in the early modern world with the verb-oriented method. In R. Sarti, A. Bellavitis, & M. Martini (Eds.), *What is work? Gender at the crossroads of home, family, and business from the early modern era to the present*. Berghahn Books (Kindle Edition).

Allen, R. (2009). *The British industrial revolution in global perspective*. Cambridge University Press.

Allen, R., Bassino, J.-P., Ma, D., Moll-Murata, C., & van Zanden, J. (2011). Wages, prices and living standards in China, 1738–1925: In comparison with Europe, Japan, and India. *Economic History Review, 64*(S1), 8–38.

Boter, C. (2020). Living standards and the life cycle: Reconstructing household income and consumption in the early twentieth-century Netherlands. *Economic History Review, 73*(4), 1050–1073.

Broadberry, S., Campbell, B., Klein, A., Overton, M., & van Leeuwen, B. (2015). *British economic growth 1270–1870*. Cambridge University Press.

Burnette, J. (2021). Why we shouldn't measure women's labour force participation in pre-industrial countries. *Economic History of Developing Regions, 36*(3), 422–427.

Burnette, J. (2024). How not to measure the standard of living: Male wages, non-market production and household income in nineteenth-century Europe. *Economic History Review, 78*(1), 87–112. https://doi.org/10.1111/ehr. 13339

De Moor, T., & van Zanden, J. (2010). 'Girl power': The European marriage pattern and labour markets in the North Sea region in the late medieval and early modern period. *Economic History Review, 63*, 1–33.

De Vries, J. (2008). *The industrious revolution: Consumer behavior and the household economy, 1650 to the present*. Cambridge University Press.

De Vries, J. (2011). Industrious peasants in East and West: Markets, technology, and family structure in Japanese and Western European agriculture. *Australian Economic History Review, 51*(2), 107–119.

Francks, P. (2016). *Japan and the Great Diveergence*. Palgrave Macmillan.

Gazeley, I. and Horrell, S. (2013). Nutrition in the English agricultural labourer's household over the course of the long nineteenth century. *Economic History Review, 66*(3), 757–784.

Griffen, E. (2010). *A short history of the British industrial revolution.* Palgrave Macmillan.

Horrell, S., Humphries, J., & Weisdorf, J. (2021). Family standards of living over the long run: England 1280–1850. *Past and Present, 250*, 87–134.

Humphries, J., & Sarasúa, C. (2012). Off the record: Reconstructing women's labor force participation in the European past. *Feminist Economics, 18*(4), 39–67.

Merouani, Y., & Perrin, F. (2022). Gender and the long-run development process: A survey of the literature. *European Review of Economic History, 26*, 612–641.

Overton, M. (1996). *Agricultural Revolution in England: the Transformaton of the Agrarian Economy 1500--1850.* Cambridge University Press.

Pomeranz, K. (2000). *The great divergence: China, Europe and the making of the modern world economy.* Princeton University Press.

Saitō, O. (2010). An industrious revolution in an East Asian market economy? Tokugawa Japan and implications for the great divergence. *Australian Economic History Review, 50*(3), 240–261.

Sarasúa, C. (2019). Women's work and structural change: Occupational structure in eighteenth-century Spain. *Economic History Review, 72*, 481–509.

Shepard, A. (2015). Crediting women in the early modern English economy. *History Workshop Journal, 79*, 1–24.

Thirsk, J. (2006). *Food in early modern England.* Continuum.

Whittle, J. (2014). Enterprising widows and active wives: Women's unpaid work in the household economy of early modern England. *History of the Family, 19*(3), 283–300.

Whittle, J. (2019). A critique of approaches to 'domestic work': Women, work and the pre-industrial economy. *Past and Present, 243*, 35–70.

Whittle, J., & Hailwood, M. (2020). The gender division of labour in early modern England. *Economic History Review, 73*(1), 3–32.

You, X. (2024). Female relatives and domestic service in nineteenth-century England and Wales: Female kin servants revisited. *Economic History Review, 77*(2), 389–471.

CHAPTER 3

The Context of Women's Work and Household Labour in Japan

Abstract What are the conditions that determine the scope and scale of unpaid household labour over the course of economic development and industrialisation? This chapter argues, on the basis of the Japanese case, that a relatively equal distribution of control over cultivated land, combined with relative security of land tenure and supported by communal institutions, created the framework within which small-scale cultivation and a high level of self-sufficiency in consumption goods persisted, in the face of the wider commercialisation and growth of the economy. This depended on the flexible availability of household labour, much of it female and individually 'unpaid'. The institutions of rural life enabled households to adjust their labour forces by means of birth control, adoption, marriage and divorce, rather than resort to the labour market. With the spread of labour-using, yield-increasing agricultural techniques and opportunities for manufacturing activity that could be fitted round them, the importance of the female members of the household labour force increased, as reflected in family planning and strategic marriage/divorce practice. As a result, Japan was able to pursue a 'housework-intensive' development path within which household-based female workers played a central, even if largely unmeasurable and unrecognised, role.

P. Francks, *Housework, Consumption and Female Labour in Japan, 1600–1940*, Palgrave Studies in Economic History,
https://doi.org/10.1007/978-3-031-83693-0_3

Keywords Food self-sufficiency in Japan · Small-scale cultivation ·
Japanese household structure · Unpaid household labour in Japan ·
Women's role in Japanese households

The previous chapter summarised available evidence that work in many
forms, over and above the labour of 'breadwinner' men, has contributed
to output and living standards in changing ways across a variety of environments experiencing economic development. By no means all these
contributions are reflected in the kinds of individual wage payment for
which historical data exist, so that the role of unpaid household labour,
typically carried out for the most part by women, in determining living
standards and welfare remains difficult to assess. This chapter uses the
Japanese case to consider what might determine the scope and nature of
that role and, in particular, which factors have influenced the extent of
unpaid labour within the household. This matters because, to the degree
that the role of unpaid labour is greater, the larger will be the under-
measurement of incomes and living standards in any given place and time.
Hence, recognition of the significance of largely unmeasurable, unpaid
labour, much of it carried out by women, in determining living standards
might lead to a re-assessment of relative levels across countries and hence
of the conditions under which industrialisation took place.

LAND AND EQUALITY

From the beginning of the seventeenth century until at least the 1920s,
Japan's economy and society were dominated by relatively small-scale
household-based units.[1] This was especially so in agriculture, but also
continued to be the case in much of manufacturing industry and services,
both rural and urban, where small-scale businesses, often organised into
supportive networks, dominated production and employment through
the pre-World War II period. Small-scale farms and businesses relied
for the most part on household-based labour, and wage-employment on
anything other than a temporary basis remained unusual until the inter-
war years at least. Better-off households did take in servants but treated
them as (inferior) household members, rewarded with board, lodging and

---

[1] For a survey of the data and literature on this, see Tanimoto (2006).

clothing, together with some form of lump-sum reward for loyal service. Marriage rates were exceptionally high, especially for women (Kurosu 2011: 119).[2] Independent existence outside a household unit of some kind remained a struggle undertaken only by vagrants, mendicant priests and other unusual individuals.

The basis for this lay, this chapter will suggest, in what was, compared to for instance much of Europe, a relatively equal distribution of control over agricultural land and its cultivation, even if the distribution of landownership was less equal. The chapter argues that this created the conditions for subsistence cultivation to continue, alongside increasing engagement with the markets for labour and goods. Unpaid household labour was crucial to the cultivation and processing of subsistence crops, while also contributing to the production of commercial crops and other goods. The supply of such labour depended on the structure of the household and its reproduction, while its productive deployment was contingent on the development of technical systems that raised the returns to land and labour within the constraints of small-scale cultivation. Meanwhile, village institutions provided a framework of support for the small-scale cultivators on whom agriculture depended. In what follows, we examine how these systems operated in the Japanese context to generate conditions conducive to a relatively large role for unpaid and often female labour as the economy grew and changed.

The basic structures of land distribution and cultivation that persisted in Japan into the twentieth century have their origins in the system of administrative control established by the government of the Tokugawa Shoguns in the early seventeenth century. Local areas outside the domains of the Shogunate itself were placed under the control of feudal lords who were empowered to levy taxes on cultivation in order to fund their military and administrative activities. The samurai warrior class, who had existed as the private armies of local lords, were deprived of the rights over land they had enjoyed and required to live around the castle of their lord, subsisting on the stipend he awarded them.

This left the feudal authorities dependent on village communities to administer the countryside and secure the taxation which constituted their

---

[2] Through the eighteenth and nineteenth centuries, most women had been married at least once before they reached the age of 30 (Kurosu, 2011: 119). By contrast, where the European Marriage Pattern prevailed, marriage tended to be late and by no means universal.

income. Taxes were levied on the village as a whole and were usually paid in kind, typically a share of the rice crop. Village institutions kept records of the land cultivated by member households and divided up the tax burden accordingly. Households did not strictly 'own' the land they managed and there was no market in landownership; rather, past history and the assumption of responsibility for tax contributions confirmed the rights and responsibilities of households over units of land. Village-level institutions continued to manage crucial aspects of the cultivation system, in particular much of the irrigation provision, and communal activities were often vital to economic survival.[3]

It is thought that, prior to the Tokugawa take-over, cultivation had typically been undertaken by extended-family groupings who managed relatively large holdings of cultivable land. However, the establishment of peace in a previously warring countryside created the conditions for the growth of towns and cities and increasing commercialisation of the production systems supplying them. In the earlier years of the Tokugawa period, it was still possible to expand or greatly improve the cultivated area through investment in drainage and irrigation systems. However, before long, given the limitations to expanding cultivation further into Japan's mountainous and forested terrain, meeting the growth in demand for rice and other commercial crops came to depend to a major extent on intensifying the cultivation of existing land. This involved investment in land improvement that created the conditions for the adoption of yield-increasing techniques such as multiple cropping and other labour-intensive methods. These proved hard to manage on the basis of an extended labour force and larger holdings were increasingly split up into units that could be managed by the three-generational nuclear family grouping known as the *ie*. As we shall see, this proved to be a rather effective system in terms of both raising land yields and engaging with growth in market demand.[4]

As a result, the small-scale farm, cultivating on the basis of family labour, became the fundamental unit of the rural economy and society, in many ways unchallenged, despite the massive upheavals in Japanese life of the nineteenth and twentieth centuries, until the era of the post-war

---

[3] For a more detailed summary, see Francks (2006, ch. 4).

[4] For the classic analysis of this process in English, see Smith (1959).

economic miracle.[5] Institutional mechanisms emerged such that those who did end up controlling more land than they could manage with available family labour were able to rent out their surplus, so that the upper stratum of village society eventually built up holdings of tenanted land that they managed alongside their own cultivation. However, their holdings as landlords—even the largest in the north-east of the country—remained tiny by comparison with elite landowners in, for example, Europe, with the majority renting out no more than a few hectares to other local farmers. Meanwhile, households with more labour than they could effectively use on any land they owned, had the option to rent in extra, thus becoming part of the class of 'owner-tenant' households that predominated in the countryside by the inter-war period.[6]

Tenancy thus proved to be a key element in enabling small-scale cultivators to adjust their land holdings to their family circumstances. Land could be rented in or out in response to the availability of labour, while cultivation rights, governed by custom, tended to be relatively secure and supported by village practice. By the inter-war period, conflict between landlords and tenant unions was emerging, but this is now recognised as a reflection of the growing strength of 'core' households, many of whom rented in land as well as owning some, in operating yield-increasing technology and engaging with the commercial market for agricultural goods (Francks, 2006: 236–243). Landlords' share of the income from the land was falling and Waswo (1977) shows how 'the decline of a rural elite' had set in well before the post-war land reform which expropriated almost all tenanted land in favour of the cultivator.

These developments are reflected in the data we do have on the distribution of households by scale of cultivation and ownership status, collected by government institutions from the early twentieth century (Table 3.1). They demonstrate that, over the 1908–1940 period, the middling group of households farming 0.5–2.0 ha occupied a slowly rising share of just over 50% of cultivating households, while households owning at least some of the land they cultivated consistently represented around 70% of the total. Hence, despite some concentration in landownership, those farming middling-scale holdings, typically partly owned and

[5] For a summary of the largely Japanese-language literature on rural institutions, see Arimoto and Sakane (2021).

[6] See Waswo (1977) for the best description of this in English.

partly rented, continued to strengthen their position as the central core of agricultural producers, recognised by the inter-war period as the key political and social force in the countryside.[7]

This meant that, as long as the household remained the basic institution of economic and social organisation, rural society in Japan remained relatively equal, in terms of access to productive assets at least, when compared with other historical examples, where the concentration of agricultural land into larger holdings, increasingly farmed in more capital-intensive ways using wage labour, has been assumed to be part of the industrialisation process. Saitō's attempt to compare pre-industrial England, India and Japan in terms of class-based income distribution concludes that Japan may have gone through the early stages of development on the basis of a significantly more equal structure, in terms of landholding, taxation and the political and economic power of a landlord or aristocratic class than observable elsewhere.[8]

Table 3.1 The distribution of households by scale of cultivation and ownership status, 1908–1940 (%)

	Households by scale of cultivation in hectares				Cultivating households by status		
	−0.5	0.5–1.0	1.0–2.0	2.0–	Owner	Owner/tenant	Tenant
1908	37.3	32.6	19.5	10.6	33.3	39.1	27.6
1912	37.2	33.2	19.6	10.0	32.5	40.0	27.5
1917	36.1	33.4	20.4	10.1	31.0	40.9	28.1
1922	35.1	33.5	21.3	10.1	30.6	41.1	28.3
1927	34.7	34.2	21.6	9.5	30.7	42.1	27.2
1932	34.0	34.3	22.2	9.5	30.5	42.7	26.8
1937	33.4	34.3	22.8	9.4	30.5	42.3	27.2
1940	33.4	32.8	24.5	9.3	30.5	42.4	27.1

Source Kayō (1958 Tables D-a-1 and E-a-1)

---

[7] For more detail, see Francks (2006: ch. 6).

[8] Saitō (2015). Saitō also interestingly links Japan's greater equality to the Tokugawa seclusion policy that limited the ability of the merchant and samurai classes to profit from international trade (415–416).

The 0.5–2 ha cultivation scale around which Japan's distribution of cultivated land tended to concentrate, as the commercial and eventually industrial economy grew, is generally acknowledged as the ideal size of farm for cultivation by a family-based household unit under Japanese conditions. Moreover, its superiority continued to be reinforced by a process of technological and institutional development that enabled output growth in support of industrialisation. In the agricultural sector, this took the form of a package of technological changes, with origins during the Tokugawa period, that centred on the establishment of multiple cropping of rice and commercial crops, supported by increasing use of commercial fertiliser and labour-intensive cultivation practices.[9] The adoption of the package demanded the high level of commitment, skill and care that only a family labour force could provide, so that attempts at larger-scale cultivation were never able to compete with the yields or the commercial and environmental flexibility that small-scale cultivators could achieve. As a result, family-based households remained the bedrock of the village and its institutions continued to develop to support small-scale owner-tenant cultivators through investment in irrigation provision, co-operative marketing, extension activities and much more.

At the same time, the seasonality of agricultural production, combined with the flexibility of family labour, could enable small-scale cultivators to take advantage of opportunities for non-farm employment which were compatible with a continued contribution to the work and income of their rural households. The expansion of manufacturing output, in textiles especially, depended on the ability of commercial merchants to organise networks of household-based producers that utilised the spare labour time of family workers, typically the female ones, on a piece-work basis (e.g. Tanimoto, 2006: 11–17). The highly labour-intensive but seasonal production of silk cocoons could be fitted into the household's work-load, especially with the introduction of silk-worm varieties that hatched during slacker periods in the agricultural cycle.[10] Household-based spinning and weaving of linen and subsequently cotton on piecework contracts met the majority of the expanding domestic demand for clothing fabrics through to the inter-war period, but many basic consumer

---

[9] For a more detailed survey, see Francks (2006, chs 2 and 3).

[10] For a description of what this involved, see Partner (2004: 17–20).

goods, and a large part of Japan's early exports after the opening to foreign trade in the 1850s, were produced within a rural economy that at the same time continued to keep the country largely self-sufficient in food.[11]

Nonetheless, by the later nineteenth century, local by-employment had ceased to represent the only form through which rural households engaged with the growing manufacturing sector. Practices of seasonal or fixed-term migration from rural areas had been common through the Tokugawa period and it was on this basis that emerging factory-based industries came to recruit the labour they required.[12] The most well-known and widely studied example of this has been the system of recruitment used by textile mills, whereby girls from rural families were hired on fixed-term contracts covering the years before they married.[13] These contracts were negotiated by the girl's parents and her wages were expected to be subsumed into the household's overall income. Hence, while in general, as in other industrialising countries, the majority of the early industrial labour force was female, income from non-agricultural work continued to be regarded as supporting the rural household, rather than as providing the means to establish an independent wage-earning existence. As the next section will suggest, 'girl power' was increasingly observable in commercialising and industrialising Japan, but it had to be manipulated within the structure of the household on which the predominant rural economy was based.[14]

Meanwhile, the household-based structure of the rural economy provided the model for business organisation more widely. As markets for goods increased during the Tokugawa period, entrepreneurs diversified on the basis of their agricultural holdings, forming branch enterprises in manufacturing and commerce that took advantage of expanding opportunities in both urban and rural areas. As a result, small-scale and often family-based businesses continued to dominate the economy, even as

---

[11] For more detailed surveys, see Francks (2006, 130–132) or Arimoto and Sakane (2021).

[12] For examples of how this worked in the (very large) prostitution industry during the Tokugawa period, see Stanley (2012).

[13] For a detailed analysis, see Hunter (2003).

[14] For an engaging real-life example see Stanley (2020) whose protagonist battles to establish a working life in Edo, away from her long-suffering family in the countryside.

new forms of industrial production developed after the Meiji Restoration of 1868. As Tanimoto's detailed analysis of Tokyo's manufacturing industry reveals, the vast majority of output was produced within small-scale workshops, reliant on the labour of the craftsman head of household, supported by his wife and children. Hired workers, often relatives of the family, could be incorporated into the household labour force as required, with a view to establishing their own workshops in due course. Such businesses formed networks producing parts for assembly, while building up the skills and relationships which were to provide the basis for the subcontracting system that characterised Japanese industry in the post-war 'miracle' period (Tanimoto, 2013).

Thus, in Japan, commercialisation and industrialisation were achieved within a structure of small-scale producers, with less concentration of income, wealth and control over land than appears to have been the case in the typical examples of such processes elsewhere. In particular, growth in the dominant rural economy resulted not in the concentration of landownership and increasingly large-scale cultivation observed in classic cases of industrialisation, but rather in a strengthening of the economic and political position of the small-scale cultivating household. Throughout the world, small-scale, family-based cultivation has offered an environment within which subsistence production and unpaid household labour can persist. In the Japanese case, as we shall see, this did not preclude growing involvement in commercial production and engagement with labour markets, where this was compatible with farm labour demands. Nonetheless, wage labour remained a largely supplementary source of income for most households until after World War II. The final section of this chapter will look at how households continued to combine their commercial activities with the possibilities for subsistence production that their relatively secure access to land facilitated, but first we need to consider the institutions of the household that supported the small-scale cultivating unit through the pre-industrial and industrialising periods.

SMALL-SCALE LANDOWNERSHIP, EMPLOYMENT AND SELF-SUFFICIENCY

It is surely the case, across the world, that small-scale cultivation, reliance on family labour and household self-sufficiency are inextricably linked, especially as regards the provision of food. Self-sufficiency generates

demand for housework which the household labour force meets; the cultivation of relatively equal, small-scale plots supports the production of
small quantities of a range of crops, suitable for home processing and
consumption. The decline of self-provisioning amidst growing reliance
on the market is a standard part of the development process but its
scope and speed have varied over time and space, seemingly dependant
on the wide range of environmental, institutional, economic and cultural
factors that determine the availability of household labour and the structure of land tenure. In Japan, the result has been a persistently high rate
of self-sufficiency, particularly in food, among the rural households that
constituted the majority until the inter-war period.

Solid data on the rates and nature of self-sufficiency are hard to come
by for early periods when it seems to have been largely taken for granted,
in the countryside at least. Households paid their rent and (up to 1871)
their taxes in kind, typically rice, and whatever grain (rice and the non-rice
grains—mainly wheat, barley, naked barley and rye—collectively known as
mugi) that remained would hopefully constitute the basis of their diet
for the year, supplemented with produce grown in vegetable gardens
and orchards, foraged or hunted or bartered with neighbours. The only
product regularly bought in was salt, although items such as dried fish
and seaweed were increasingly available from village shops and travel-
ling sales-people. Areas of commercial market-gardening were emerging
around the major conurbations by the second half of the Tokugawa
period and specialised cultivation of industrial crops such as sugar-cane,
mulberry (for silkworms) and mat-rush were developing where conditions were appropriate. However, the default position for the majority
of households continued to involve more-or-less complete reliance on
home-grown produce to meet consumption needs.

For the inter-war period we do have some data that confirm the scale
and persistence of rural self-sufficiency into the period of industrialisation,
as summarised in Table 3.2. These data come from a series of surveys
undertaken by agricultural officials among rural households during the
1920s, generally known as the Farm Household Economy Surveys (Nōka
Keizai Chōsa). Not much is known about how participants were selected,
but it is likely, as is usually the case with such surveys, that officials
were biased towards the 'core' householders they knew, who were more
likely to be able to understand and complete the survey documents. The
published data are divided according to tenancy status, broadly reflecting

the distribution of income and power within the village.[15] The average size of cultivated holding among surveyed households was 1.5–2 ha and average household size ranged from 6.5 to 7.5 persons, with owners at the top of the range on both counts and pure-tenants at the bottom, although the differences are small. Income and expenses in kind were valued according to prevailing market prices.

Table 3.2 (Part A) shows the share of total household expenditure made in kind, that is to say from their own cultivation and production, possibly supplemented by some exchange with neighbours. For all types of household, at least 40% of their total expenses was recorded as being in kind over the 1921–1930 period and over 80% of their food.[16] This picture is confirmed in the data Embree was able to assemble covering a range of hamlets within the village of Suye in the 1930s, which show virtually all households self-sufficient in the grain they consumed (rice or *mugi*) and similarly in vegetables, pulses, soy-sauce and miso (Embree 1964, Table 10). This suggests that, across the board, rural households relied on their own cultivation for the vast majority of their food supply, even if the market was coming to supply more-and-more of their other needs.

Table 3.2 (part B) shows the recorded distribution of work activities among agriculture, housework and by-employment. The 'by-employment' category was restricted to paid activities outside the household, so that time spent on home-based by-employments, such as raising silk cocoons, was included under 'agriculture'. What is striking is that households were devoting at least a third of their labour time to what they categorised as housework. Chapter 4 will describe a number of the labour-intensive processes whereby home-grown produce was converted into meals for the household, generating a significant portion of the demand for housework which the surveys appear to suggest. The implication is that housework and self-sufficiency were inextricably linked, as family labour was mobilised to produce the final consumption goods on which the household relied. As the next section describes, beneath this lay the institutional structure of the household and the village that was to

---

[15] This in turn reflects the preoccupation, in the media, intelligentsia and officialdom of the inter-war years, with landlord/tenant, class-based conflict and the perception of rural poverty and over-population.

[16] For more detail, see Table 1 of Francks (2021).

Table 3.2 Farm Household Economy Survey Data on Self-Sufficiency and Housework, 1924–1930

A. *Shares of household expenses made in kind (%)*

	Owners		Owner-tenants		Tenants	
	Share of total expenses in kind	Share of food acquired in kind	Share of total expenses in kind	Share of food acquired in kind	Share of total expenses in kind	Share of food acquired in kind
1924	42.3	n.a	41.5	n.a	50.8	n.a
1925	40.3	83.9	42.4	83.2	46.3	77.7
1926	39.6	82.6	44.7	82.5	46.9	78.0
1927	41.9	81.5	45.5	83.2	47.9	80.8
1928	39.3	81.6	42.8	81.9	46.7	80.0
1929	37.7	81.0	42.6	81.3	43.4	78.4
1930	40.6	81.3	44.3	81.4	47.7	81.2

B. *Distribution of hours worked by activity (%)*

	Owners			Owner-tenants			Tenants		
	Agriculture	By-employment	Housework	Agriculture	By-employment	Housework	Agriculture	By-employment	Housework
1924	53.7	5.9	40.4	53.7	5.4	39.2	54.7	10.0	35.3
1925	54.3	4.1	41.6	56.9	5.2	37.0	57.3	9.8	32.9
1926	55.3	4.6	40.0	57.2	5.2	38.1	53.9	8.5	37.6
1927	57.5	5.2	37.3	58.7	5.5	34.0	60.9	8.0	31.2
1928	55.3	5.3	39.4	58.6	5.3	33.1	56.8	8.6	34.6
1929	56.3	5.2	38.4	57.9	5.3	34.6	57.0	8.5	34.5
1930	58.7	4.6	36.7	60.0	5.3	32.9	61.1	6.8	32.2

Source Data from two series of Farm Household Economy Surveys made by the Ministry of Agriculture and Forestry (1921–1923 and 1924–1930), as reproduced in Inaba (1953: 46–47 and 56–57) support the small-scale cultivating unit and its self-sufficiency throughout the pre-industrial and industrialising period.

FAMILY STRUCTURE, SMALL-SCALE CULTIVATION AND UNPAID LABOUR

The previous sections have portrayed the economy of pre-industrial and industrialising Japan as dominated by small-scale household-based producers, a substantial proportion of whom continued to practise a relatively high degree of self-sufficiency, especially in food. This section considers the ways in which this was reflected in household structures and the organisation of production activities, especially as regards unpaid work and female labour. As we have seen, with the break-up of extended-family households controlling relatively large holdings, the organisation of cultivation fell into the hands of the smaller, family-based units better able to manage intensive cultivation under Japanese conditions. In fact, such units depended on support from wider institutions, including group-ings based on family links and communal village structures, but the day-to-day productive activities of the household were the responsibility of the current household head. The village was regarded as made up of individual households endowed with rights and responsibilities in return for support and protection. The resulting structures and institu-tions largely persisted, despite government attempts at rationalisation and modernisation, through to the post-war land reform if not further.

There were undoubtedly variations over time and across the country in the customs that governed family organisation within the household. However, through the course of the Tokugawa period, households grad-ually seem to have adopted as the ideal model the so-called *ie* system, whereby the headship of the family, and responsibility for its welfare and assets through time, passed from father to eldest son, if at all possible.[17] This was not imposed by state or religious institutions, though both provided recognition and support, and was adaptable, through practices such as adoption, divorce and selective birth control, to the changing circumstances of the household. Exactly why the *ie* became the

---

[17] For more detail on the *ie*, see Berry and Yonemoto (2019). The *ie* structure spread from the samurai class to all other status groups during the first half of the Tokugawa period, and Berry and Yonemoto (2019: 7) conclude that it was a majority practice by the turn of the eighteenth century.

accepted norm, as regards family formation, from the Tokugawa period and through to quite recent times, is not clear (see Berry & Yonemoto, 2019: 9–13), and its practices were by no means costless in terms of the physical and emotional burdens placed on family members. But, above all, from an economic point of view, the value placed on preserving the *ie* and its assets through time provided social and spiritual support for the maintenance of even small-scale agricultural holdings in the hands of cultivating households and to what Berry and Yonemoto (2019: 10) call 'a conflation of reputable standing with continuity over time'.

In practical terms, the establishment of an *ie* meant that, in the interests of the survival of the main household, siblings of the inheriting head were expected to find employment of their own and in the case of sisters to marry out. Where the household head did not produce a son to inherit, it was common to adopt in a daughter's husband or the 'spare' son of a related household to take on the role and adoption, by no means always based on blood relationships, was widely used as a means of ensuring succession to the headship and survival for the household line. Households were thus ideally composed of the household head and his wife, their inheriting successors and their children. Retired grandparents typically remained members of the household, creating a three-generation nuclear structure. Flexibility was provided by the possibility of renting land in/out, as we have seen, and through the labour contributions of younger sons and daughters prior to marriage, together with, if necessary, hired-in workers.

Within the *ie* structure, therefore, the core labour force of the household was composed of the household head, his wife and their successors who were responsible for cultivating and maintaining the family's holding. Little is known about how households allocated tasks or distributed income among themselves but clearly the household worked and consumed as a unit under the management of the head couple. Even when younger members of the household went out to work seasonally or on contracts their earnings were typically paid into the household pot (Hunter, 2003: 79–83). Thus the work of individual members of the household was not reflected in individual incomes or consumption and was 'unpaid' according to the 'third-party' definition outlined in the Introduction.

The income of the household—typically from cultivation of the land it controlled, together with any supplementary earnings on or off the farm—was received in cash or kind and used to meet the demands on it, including the consumption requirements (mainly food and clothing) of members, together with payments for taxes, farm inputs and investments, educational and medical expenses and so on.[18] Given that a large proportion of households continued to have access to land to cultivate for their own needs, it is clear that, as the previous section demonstrated, a substantial proportion of income was typically taken in the form of subsistence produce, grown, processed and prepared by household members.

The allocation of work tasks within the household appears to have been based, to some extent at least, on status and gender, as well as physical abilities.[19] However, given that, for the majority of households, much productive work was based in the home, the whole labour force—men and women, old and young—could easily be mobilised as required. Heavy agricultural labour was clearly the responsibility of male household members, as was commercial craft-work, but it appears to have been normal for men to assist with cooking and food processing at times (Sand, 2003: 65–67). The processing and preparation of home-grown items demanded, as we shall see in Chapter 4, a substantial input of labour and skill, which was typically supplied by female members, while childcare and the general management of the household were also women's responsibilities, assisted by older children and grandparents. However, alongside their household activities, women clearly made a substantial contribution to the agricultural work of rural households, given the demands of intensive agricultural production and the limitations on the available labour force. In particular, women were central to the capacity to meet peak labour demands in agriculture, particularly at rice-transplanting and harvesting times. In due course, as market-based opportunities expanded with the commercialisation of the economy, women took on a major share of the labour involved in textile production within the home and eventually contract work in the emerging textile mills of the nineteenth century. It was essentially through the flexibility of women's paid and unpaid labour for the household that the rural sector of the economy was enabled

[18] For the budget of a very poor household in the 1930s, see Partner (2004: 20–21).

[19] For useful summaries of the division of household activities in pre-war rural and urban households, see Uno (1991). Tanimoto (2012) analyses available statistical data from surveys covering the early twentieth century.

to respond to the opportunities presented by economic growth and industrialisation, while maintaining a structure of small-scale, labour-intensive land management.

This is reflected in the growing evidence that, from the later Tokugawa period onwards, girls were coming to be regarded as relatively valuable assets to a family. It is now accepted that by then households were seeking to control the size and gender distribution of their membership, through birth control measures that included infanticide. However, Drixler, in his study of the practice in northeastern Japan during the eighteenth and nineteenth centuries, shows that families' management of household composition was more complex than simple bias against girls, involving consideration of not just the size but also the appropriate sex distribution of the household head's children (Drixler, 2013: ch 6). Families recognised that they needed both boys and girls, if they were to meet their labour requirements, as well as their reproductive objectives. Young girls provided crucial assistance to their mothers around the house and in child-minding, as well as in textile-related activities. Older daughters, prior to marriage, constituted a major element in the hired labour force, going out to work on what was assumed to be a temporary basis in domestic service, prostitution and eventually textile workshops and factories.

The labour of daughters was eventually lost to their natal households on marriage. For the households into which they married, however, their role as successor to their mother-in-law in the management of the household, and their contribution of, hopefully, relatively young and fit labour, would have been crucial to small-scale cultivating households and there is evidence of growing concern over the choice of incoming brides for succeeding sons. Marriage became the key mechanism for achieving 'optimal household size and the gender balance of labor for family farming' (Kurosu, 2011: 119). The ability to contribute to the available labour of their husband's household, as well as to fit into its economic and social structure, was central to marriage choices, but equally the increasing importance of her contribution to the labour force must have strengthened the traditionally weak position of the successor's bride. The conflicts involved in this process were reflected in the remarkably high divorce rate that had emerged by the nineteenth century, as brides and families tried to adapt to each other, under conditions where female labour was crucial to household fortunes.[20]

Meanwhile urban households, at least in the dominant small-scale sector, continued to adopt the same structure and practices as rural ones, as far as they could. The scope for subsistence production of food was naturally much more limited than in the countryside, but women clearly contributed in other ways to the activities of small-scale businesses in manufacturing, services and commerce in the towns and cities. Since the labour force in such businesses almost always lived in, the provision of food and clothing for workers would have been the housewife's responsibility. Wives entertained customers and business associates, managed day-to-day expenses, and served alongside their husbands in shops and craft workshops. By the inter-war period, male white- and blue-collar employment in larger-scale establishments was expanding and where it paid enough, opened up scope for the emergence of the modern 'specialist' housewife. However, for most women this was a model to which they might aspire but far from the day-to-day reality of work to support their husband's business and the welfare of the household (Tanimoto, 2013).

Altogether, therefore, the institutional structures of the rural and, to a large extent, urban economies of commercialising and industrialising Japan provided an ideal environment for the deployment of unpaid labour (male and female) within the household. Marriage, supplemented by adoption, rather than recourse to the wage-labour market, represented the key institutional mechanism for adjusting labour demand and supply within the household, with the result that most work was carried out by household members. Such activity was 'unpaid', in the sense that it was not rewarded by payments to individuals, and except where it resulted in commercial output, its contribution to GDP would not have left a record. Chapter 4 will examine the nature of that contribution in more detail but first we can close this chapter by using the Japanese case to consider how

---

[20] See for example Kurosu (2011). In the northeastern villages whose records for 1716–1870 Kurosu studied, more than two-thirds of first marriages ended in divorce before the couple reached fifty (p. 118). 'Spousal testing' in the first few years of marriage was common and helps to account for the high divorce rate among younger couples. Tsuneno, the subject of Amy Stanley's recent study, was married and divorced three times (mostly at her own instigation), as she sought to find a place for herself within the changing Tokugawa world (Stanley, 2020).

the relatively widespread availability of household labour might have influenced the pattern of development in the wider economy and society over time.

HOUSEHOLD LABOUR AND THE PATTERN OF JAPANESE ECONOMIC DEVELOPMENT

By the time of World War II, Japan had become an industrial power capable of challenging the developed countries of the period, both commercially and militarily. However, this had been achieved on an institutional and structural basis quite different from that assumed to have supported industrialisation in northern Europe. In particular, modernising Japan remained a society in which the family-based household represented the key institution in the organisation of economic and social life. This was particularly so in the rural sector, where the management of agriculture remained in the hands of small-scale cultivating households, but was also the case, as we have seen, in large parts of the manufacturing and services sectors, where small-scale producers continued to dominate. By the inter-war period, large-scale business organisations were establishing themselves; full-time wage-employment was becoming more common, and the practices that sustained the traditional household, in relation to marriage and family life in general, were beginning to be challenged, as younger people gradually found ways to support themselves independently of their natal households. Nonetheless, the influence of a long-term pattern of development based on the household was already well embedded, generating economic and social structures rather different from those that characterise the model of industrialisation in 'the West'.[21] These structures provided scope for the utilisation of unpaid household labour on a relatively large scale, even within an industrialising economy, if the means could be found to achieve it.

It might be expected that the main impact of the relatively widespread availability of household labour would be found on the consumption and labour-market sides of the economy. It is indeed the case that a number of scholars have pointed out the relatively slow rate of commercialisation

---

[21] In fact, it is not difficult to find examples of industrial growth in household-dominated societies in Europe—northern Italy is a classic example.

and market penetration that accompanied Japanese economic growth.[22] Rural households in particular remained almost entirely self-sufficient in food into the inter-war period and continued to be able to meet most of their consumption requirements without recourse to the market, even where their demands were changing. In their 'unpaid' workers, households possessed resources of labour and skill that markets could not tap but which contributed in unmeasurable ways to their living standards and welfare.

Meanwhile, however, the availability of household labour can be argued to have affected the production side of the economy as well. Maximising the living standards of the household meant, on the one hand, adjusting its membership/labour force to its stock of land and capital and, on the other hand, finding productive ways to mobilise its labour resources as fully as possible. The former could be achieved through family planning, combined with use of social connections that enabled workers to move in and out of their natal households by means of adoption, marriage and divorce. The latter depended on the development of techniques and organisational forms suited to a labour force of varying ages and abilities based within the household. Although in some ways parallel to the 'labour-intensive path' that many have argued Japan followed (e.g. Sugihara, 2013), the resulting 'housework-intensive' path has distinctive characteristics of its own and important implications for our understanding of changing living standards and gender roles as industrialisation occurred.

In relation to Japanese agriculture, analysis of the 'labour-intensive path' of technical and organisational change is long-standing. The increases in agricultural output that met much of the growing demand for food generated by population increase and rising incomes in town and country were achieved through yield-increasing methods that included intensive use of fertiliser, multiple cropping made possible by investment in irrigation systems, and a range of improved cultivation methods requiring care and attention, as well as hours of labour.[23] Although men typically carried out the heavy work on the farm, such as ploughing and preparing fields for planting, other tasks, including caring for seed-beds

[22] The slow rate of commercialisation in Japan is the reason why de Vries (2011) concludes that there cannot have been an 'industrious revolution' of the form he describes.

[23] For the classic account, see Smith (1959: ch 7). For a more recent summary, Francks (2006: 26–36, 139–143).

and transplanting, as well as harvesting, traditionally involved substantial amounts of female labour, while much of the work of processing crops after harvest fell to women.

It follows that the adoption of yield-increasing methods required the mobilisation of the entire household labour force. The utilisation of improved techniques placed new demands on the female labour force in agriculture—larger harvests to process, for instance. It was possible to accommodate this without hiring extra labour if other household members could be organised to perform the activities that might otherwise have fallen to core female workers. Grandmothers cooked and tended vegetable plots; older children minded their younger siblings and fetched firewood and water. Adoption of the labour-intensive path of agricultural development thus hinged on the ability to utilise the labour of female household members (and children), much of whose work and contribution to overall output remains unrecorded.[24]

Similar processes must have occurred to accommodate the growth of production in manufacturing industries, notably textiles. Textiles remained by far the most important non-food manufacturing industry in terms of output and exports throughout Japan's pre-war industrialisation and the vast majority of the textile labour force was female. Silk, ramie and later cotton were traditionally spun and woven within the household to supply clothing needs and if possible to market. As demand for textiles increased through the nineteenth century, household-based production remained the bedrock of the industry, meeting the bulk of domestic demand for the Japanese-style clothing materials that most consumers continued to use.[25] Putting-out systems became common, with textile merchants supplying raw materials to household-based spinners and weavers and collecting the finished product to market, in return for cash or a share of output. Such networks proved capable of responding to changes in both available technology and inputs— new types of loom, expanding supplies of cotton—and in consumer tastes, as merchant-organisers sought to maintain quality within increasingly fashion-conscious markets. By the later nineteenth century, factory production was becoming established in certain branches of the industry,

---

[24] For more detail on the household work involved, see ch 4.

[25] This relies on the large body of work in Japanese by Takeshi Abe. For more detail, see Tanimoto (2006) and for a summary in English, see Francks (2015).

particularly cotton-spinning and silk reeling, with younger daughters of rural households supplying the wage labour required, as we have seen. However, household-based workers, most of them women, remained central to textile production for the growing home market and putting-out systems mobilising the labour time of women in rural households were also utilised in a range of other lines of production supplying domestic and export markets.[26]

Where marketed or paid for in cash the output of household-based workers would theoretically be recognised in estimates of GDP. However, as with women's contributions to growing labour requirements in agriculture, increased hours of, for instance, spinning or weaving by core workers depended on the mobilisation of the whole household to fulfil the housework tasks necessary to subsistence and welfare. Hence, for instance, children are often recorded as assisting with subsidiary tasks in spinning and weaving, as well as a whole range of household tasks (Uno, 1991: 34–35). The critical contribution of this unpaid work to the ability of the household to raise its income and living standard cannot be measured but must have been significant, as details in the next chapter illustrate. At the same time, it was also vital to the persistence of the small-scale producing household, in agriculture and to a degree elsewhere, as it sought to respond to the commercialisation and industrialisation of the economy.

* * *

This chapter has outlined the institutional and economic factors that made the 'housework-intensive' development path feasible under Japanese conditions. Although impossible to quantify, the unpaid labour of household members, especially women, was crucial to the ability of small-scale household production to grow and support the industrialisation process. The ability to mobilise unpaid labour as and when required provided the flexibility that enabled workers to diversify their activities, while ensuring the day-to-day welfare and reproduction of the whole household. The next chapter will consider the actual content of unpaid household activities and the pattern of consumption that they generated, as incomes rose and Japan developed into a modern industrial society.

[26] For examples, see Takeuchi (1991).

REFERENCES

Arimoto, Y., & Sakane, Y. (2021). Agricultural development in industrialising Japan, 1880–1940. *Australian Economic History Review, 61*(3), 290–317. https://doi.org/10.1111/aehr.12223

Berry, M., & Yonemoto, M. (2019). Introduction. In M. Berry & M. Yonemoto (Eds.), *What is a family? Answers from early modern Japan* (pp. 1–20). University of California Press. https://doi.org/10.1525/luminos.77

De Vries, J. (2011). Industrious peasants in East and West: Markets, technology, and family structure in Japanese and Western European agriculture. *Australian Economic History Review, 51*(2), 107–119.

Drixler, F. (2013). *Mabiki: Infanticide and population growth in eastern Japan, 1660–1950*. University of California Press.

Embree, J. (1964). *Suye Mura: a Japanese Village*. University of Chicago Press.

Francks, P. (2006). *Rural economic development in Japan: From the nineteenth century to the Pacific war*. Routledge.

Francks, P. (2015). Was fashion a European invention? The kimono and economic development in Japan. *Fashion Theory, 19*(3), 331–361. https://doi.org/10.2752/175174115X14223685749368

Francks, P. (2021). Industriousness and divergence: Living standards, housework and the Japanese diet in comparative historical perspective. *Australian Economic History Review, 1–21.* https://doi.org/10.1111/aehr.12222

Hunter, J. (2003). *Women and the labour market in Japan's industrialising economy: The textile industry before the Pacific war*. Routledge Curzon.

Inaba, T. (1953). *Nōka Keizai Chōsa Hōkoku: Chōsa Hōhō no Hensen to Ruinen Seiseki* (A report on the farm household economy survey: Changes in survey methods and statistical series). Nōrinshō Nōgyō Sōgō Kenkyūjo.

Kayō, N. (1958). *Nihon Nōgyō Kiso Tōkei* (Basic statistics of Japanese agriculture). Nōrinsuisangyō Seisansei Kōjō Kaigi.

Kurosu, S. (2011). Divorce in early modern rural Japan: Household and individual life course in Northeastern villages, 1716–1870. *Journal of Family History, 36*(2), 118–141.

Partner, S. (2004). *Toshié: a Story of Village Life in Twentieth-Century Japan*. University of California Press.

Saitō, O. (2015). Growth and inequality in the great and little divergence debate. *Economic History Review, 68*(2), 399–419.

Sand, J. (2003). *House and home in modern Japan: Architecture, domestic space, and bourgeois culture, 1880–1930*. Harvard University Press.

Smith, T. C. (1959). *The agrarian origins of modern Japan*. Stanford University Press.

Stanley, A. (2012). *Selling women: Prostitution, markets, and the household in early modern Japan*. University of California Press.

Stanley, A. (2020). *Stranger in the shogun's city: A woman's life in nineteenth-century Japan*. Chatto & Windus.

Sugihara, K. (2013). Labour-intensive industrialization in global history: An interpretation of East Asian experiences. In G. Austin & K. Sugihara (Eds.), *Labour-intensive industrialization in global history* (pp. 20–64). Routledge.

Takeuchi, J. (1991). *The role of labour-intensive sectors in Japanese industrialization*. United Nations University Press.

Tanimoto, M. (2006). The role of tradition in Japan's industrialization: Another path to industrialization. In M. Tanimoto (Ed.), *The role of tradition in Japan's industrialization: Another path to industrialization* (pp. 1–44). Oxford University Press.

Tanimoto, M. (2012). The role of housework in everyday life; another aspect of consumption in modern Japan. In P. Francks & J. Hunter (Eds.), *The historical consumer: Consumption and everyday life in Japan, 1850–2000* (pp. 27–55). Palgrave Macmillan.

Tanimoto, M. (2013). From peasant economy to urban agglomeration: The transformation of 'labour-intensive industrialisation' in Japan. In G. Austin & K. Sugihara (Eds.), *Labour-intensive industrialization in global history* (pp. 144–175). Routledge.

Uno, K. (1991). Women and changes in the household division of labor. In G. Bernstein (Ed.), *Recreating Japanese women, 1600–1945* (pp. 17–41). University of California Press.

Waswo, A. (1977). *Japanese landlords: The decline of a rural elite*. University of California Press.

CHAPTER 4

Housework and the Nature of Consumption Goods

Abstract Very little data, either quantitative or qualitative, exists to demonstrate the content and nature of household labour over the course of Japan's development. This chapter attempts to use what we know of the characteristics of Japanese consumer goods to derive the nature of their production and the likely contribution of female household labour to the process. Small-scale cultivation, and the high rate of household self-sufficiency in agricultural goods that it facilitated, meant that the production, processing and cooking of home-grown food made heavy demands on household labour but generated the housework-intensive forms of production that have come to characterise Japanese cuisine. Although home-production of textiles themselves largely disappeared with the growing availability of factory-made cotton cloth, the nature of the Japanese-style clothing that continued to prevail until after World War II meant lengthy and skilled work in sewing remained a significant task for the female household labour force. For the inter-war period, as Chapter 3 demonstrated, such quantitative information as we possess confirms the correlation between rising living standards and the persistent deployment of unpaid household labour, in the context of the Japanese consumption pattern.

© The Author(s), under exclusive license to Springer Nature   47
Switzerland AG 2025
P. Francks, *Housework, Consumption and Female Labour in Japan,*
1600–1940, Palgrave Studies in Economic History,
https://doi.org/10.1007/978-3-031-83693-0_4

Keywords Dietary history in Japan · Sewing in Japan ·
'Housework-intensive' development · Japanese cooking methods ·
Characteristics of Japanese consumption goods

The great difficulty involved in locating historical evidence, especially in quantifiable form, of the productive labour of female and unpaid household workers has led to some ingenious use of a range of sources which detail, for other purposes, activities carried out at any given time.[1] These provide essentially supply-side glimpses of the nature and extent of otherwise unrecorded work in the past. However, the issue could also be approached from the demand or consumption side of economic activity, through consideration of the characteristics of consumer goods and their implications for the work that must have gone into producing them. Different consumption patterns will be associated with different forms of work and hence potentially offer different scope for the deployment of household labour in production activities. Unpicking this relationship in the Japanese case requires examination of the features of consumer goods, many of which continue to be consumed to this day, and our knowledge of how they have been made in the past. This can be used to suggest the ways in which different paths of change in consumption patterns and living standards were, or became, more or less 'housework-intensive' than those of international comparators on the basis of the availability of household labour.

In this context, the Japanese case is particularly interesting, given that distinctive forms of diet, clothing and household goods have prevailed over a very long period extending through the course of Japan's economic development and industrialisation. In recent years, various Japanese consumer goods—notably food items—have entered the world of global consumption, but this was not previously the case, so that the Japanese consumption pattern, up to the late nineteenth century at least, evolved along a path largely determined by domestic conditions on both the supply and demand sides.[2] As the previous chapter

[1] E.g reports of court cases in Shepard (2015); linguistic analysis in Ågren (2018).

[2] Some consumption items can be traced back to the trade contacts between Japan and Western countries, notably Portugal, in the early seventeenth century, but these largely ceased with the 'closing' of the country by Tokugawa Ieyasu in the early seventeenth

has explained, these conditions were inter-twined with the structure and technology of household-based production that determined the scope for unpaid household labour in the production of consumer goods. From the late nineteenth century onwards, Western-style goods and the techniques that produced them began to filter into the world of Japanese everyday life, but the basic structures of ordinary consumption remained in place for most households, while new products, manufactured in new ways, were utilised for the most part as peripheral or fashionable treats and accessories.[3]

Subsequent sections therefore focus on the everyday goods, in particular food and clothing, that constituted the basis of the consumption pattern in most Japanese households through to World War II. They present qualitative evidence of the content of the work that went into their manufacture and demonstrate the degree to which elements of both the production and consumption of consumer goods might have been such as to evade standard quantitative techniques. Such evidence can then be used to throw light on the extent to which Japan followed a 'housework-intensive' path, in comparison with other parts of the developed world, with the implication that living standards, as reflected in GDP per capita, for example, might have been under-estimated in standard measurements to a greater extent in the case of Japan than elsewhere. Moreover, the everyday products which Japanese households produced and consumed over the course of their history are precisely those that have in recent years entered global consumption, so that supermarket and restaurant customers the world over are now enjoying products whose characteristics result from the unrecognised labour and skills of Japanese households pursuing their 'housework-intensive' path over the centuries.

THE FOOD SUPPLY

As in other pre-industrial and industrialising countries, food represented the largest item in the Japanese 'consumption basket' until relatively recent times. However, since the majority of the pre-World War II population continued to live in rural areas and to have access to at least some

century. Chinese influences of course persisted in some fields, such as textile design and traditional medicines, and some trade with the rest of Asia continued, despite the 'closed country' policy.

[3] For more detail, see Francks (2009: ch 4).

land to cultivate, many households continued to possess the capacity to grow a considerable part of their food for themselves if they chose to.[4] As we saw in Chapter 3, this enabled most rural households to supply almost all their food themselves, even if, by the inter-war period they were buying a growing range of items, including some commercial food products such as soy-sauce.

There exist various qualitative studies confirming that, still in the inter-war period, in rural areas, household-level self-supply of most food remained the rule. The prosperous farm family described by Bernstein relied on their own food throughout the pre-World War II period, even as they developed commercial interests such as tobacco farming and were able to hire servants to do much of the work on the farm and in the house (Bernstein, 2005: 67–68). At the other end of the social scale, as late as the 1930s, the rural family described by Partner, who put together as best a living as they could from a range of sources, continued to grow most of their own food on the small holding they rented (Partner, 2004: 10). As outlined in chapter 3 Embree's study of the village of Suye in the 1930s provides detailed data on the self-sufficiency rate for all kinds of household, broken down by food categories (Embree, 1964: appendix table 10). In general, virtually all rural households were self-sufficient in the grain that constituted the largest element in their diets, whether this was rice or 'lesser' grains, such as barley and millet. Most also relied almost exclusively on their own cultivation of beans and vegetables, enabling them to produce the majority of their pickles, miso and other flavourings. The sugar and salt necessary for these processes represented the only significant inputs into the production of their food for which households universally depended on the market.

For earlier periods, the degree of reliance on home-grown food must have been greater the further back one goes. Qualitative accounts occasionally confirm this: Kikue Yamakawa's description of life in a lower-level samurai household in the late Tokugawa period describes even this elite (though not rich) family engaging in the cultivation and processing of

---

[4] Taeuber's standard estimates show the proportion of the population living in places with fewer than 10,000 inhabitants standing at just under 90% in the 1880s and only gradually declining to reach just under 70% by 1918. Urbanisation was much faster during the inter-war period, so that almost half of the population were living in places with more than 10,000 residents by 1940. Taueber (1958: 49, 71). For a summary, see Francks (2006: Table 5.2).

a range of crops grown on the vegetable plot allocated to them by their lord (Yamakawa, 2001) Their samurai stipend was received in rice, so they did not need to cultivate this themselves, and in fact sold most of what they received to raise cash. But even the samurai head of the household helped out with the cultivation of the vegetable plot that supplied the other elements of their diet. The detailed surveys of food consumption in two late Tokugawa/early Meiji regions in the south-western domain of Chōshū which Gotō has assembled and analysed reveal a remarkably wide range of crops cultivated or foraged, the majority of which must have been destined for home consumption.[5]

Nonetheless, grains remained the most important crops grown and it is possible to make historical estimates of areas cultivated, yields and hence output of the major grain crops on which estimates of GDP can be based. The taxes that feudal rulers were able to levy on the villages of their domains were as a rule payable in rice (usually as *genmai*— hulled but not polished), so that a significant portion of the rice crop was used by the feudal ruling classes to meet their staple food requirements and as the means to raise cash to pay for their money expenses (which were substantial). Sales of tax rice led to the emergence of a national-level rice market and rice became essentially a commercial crop. In the villages, feudal taxation was traditionally levied in the form of a share of the village's rice crop and rents were typically paid in rice. By the late Tokugawa period, payments in cash or non-rice crops were spreading in more commercialised regions and the Land Tax Reform of 1873 established a cash-based taxation system which drove cultivators further into the market for rice and other crops. However, wherever rice could be grown, whatever remained after necessary payments and sales had been made constituted the basis of the household's food supply for the year. For everyday food purposes, this was widely supplemented with *mugi* grains, which could be grown on paddy-fields in the winter and on the un-irrigated upland fields that most households also cultivated, and areas of the country where rice could not be grown also necessarily relied on

---

[5] Gotō's analysis of the survey data is only published in Japanese (Gotō 2015). For more details, see Francks (2021).

mugi grains. As with rice, it has been possible to make historical estimates of *mugi* output to include in measures of GDP and living standards.[6]

Such estimates are not, however, capable of reflecting the results of household labour devoted to processing and preparing home-grown grain. Households threshed and hulled their grain themselves or in groups, using basic and generally hand-powered tools. These were improved over time, but, as Smith (1959: 102) points out, innovations such as the comb-like threshing device called the *semba-kōki*, which speeded up and lightened the task, generally freed adult labour for other work, such as planting a second crop, and enabled the mobilisation of child labour at a peak time of the year. Rice polishing to achieve the pure white grain in demand in the cities generally required the equipment and skills of specialists but was not necessary for the everyday rice boiled in stews with other grains in rural households. By the inter-war period, commercial grain hullers, using electric or water-driven machinery, had been set up in villages such as Suye (Embree, 1964: 54) but until then households had continued to hull their own grain, using unrecorded household labour time. This would appear to contrast with many parts of Europe, where bread-eating households were taking their grain to commercial wind- or water-powered mills (whose output should be included in GDP estimates) from much earlier.[7]

Meanwhile, household labour was also vital for the production of the wide range of fruit, vegetables and herbs that made predominantly grain-based meals edible and nutritious. Rural households almost universally maintained plots of land on which they grew an assortment of crops for their own use, the output of which, as Hanley (1997: 90) notes, must have been 'considerable' and unrecorded in standard data used to estimate GDP. Moreover, dietary evidence is accumulating to suggest that, as incomes and productivity rose from the later Tokugawa period onwards, the variety of such crops was expanding with the introduction of new items such as the sweet potato, improving the quality and variety of everyday meals. Hunting and fishing were also practised wherever possible, although quantities of meat consumed were small. Later, in

---

[6] The most recent and definitive estimates are assembled in Bassino et al. (2019). Historical estimates of GDP per capita (for Japan and elsewhere) are widely debated—for a survey see Francks (2016, ch 4).

[7] For an interesting discussion of the characteristics of wheat bread that made it essentially a commercial product produced by specialist bakers, see Collins (1993).

the inter-war period, Embree records Suye households as still cultivating or collecting a large range of fruit and vegetable items according to season (Embree, 1964: 42–43).[8]

At the same time, in much of the country, villages continued to maintain access to local forests and common land and these were extensively foraged, not just for firewood and fertiliser materials but also for nuts, berries, mushrooms and medicinal plants, as well as trapped and hunted wildlife. In pre-war Hida, in the south-western prefecture of Chōshū, it has been estimated that nuts (chestnuts, acorns and horse chestnuts) produced the equivalent of a quarter of the amount of rice and millet consumed, filling a crucial gap in the supply of basic foodstuff. However, this was only possible as a result of the very labour-intensive process of preparation required to render the nuts edible and in a condition to be ground and mixed with grain (Rath, 2016: 209). Nonetheless, neither the labour that went into such activities nor the contribution that they made to the sustainability of living standards have been recorded.

As a result, although it may be possible to measure the output of cultivated paddy and upland fields, for home consumption and sale, the work that went into their cultivation is only part of the story. Unrecorded production of a wide range of fruit and vegetable crops, alongside collecting and foraging, supplied vital elements of the diet, in both quantitative and qualitative terms. This involved a seasonal round of work for the entire family labour force, but was only, as we can go on to see, the first stage towards placing on the table the home-made food items that constituted the Japanese diet through much of the period up to World War II and beyond.

Processing and Cooking

As more recent literature on housework has revealed, even for developed countries few of the food ingredients that come into the household are ready for consumption without substantial preparation. This will be all the

---

[8] One type of work that Japanese households generally did not have to supply, however, involved the care of animals for food purposes. While European households continued, where they could, to keep cows, goats, pigs and chickens for their own use, Japanese households rarely consumed farmed meat and, even less so, dairy products, until the impact of Western tastes began to be felt in the inter-war period. Draught animals did have to be cared for, however, although their use is thought to have been declining, as agriculture intensified.

more so with home-grown food which needs processing, preserving and storing as well as cooking. To the extent that the results of these processes are consumed within the household and never sold, the unpaid household labour that went into them will also go unrecorded, while the quality of the products themselves will surely be higher than is reflected in the measurable value of the known inputs. This is of course the case wherever self-sufficient food production takes place. To argue that Japan followed a more 'housework-intensive' path than other industrialising countries it is therefore necessary to show, not just that self-sufficiency was more widespread and persisted longer than elsewhere, but also that the characteristics of final food products could only be produced as a result of high levels of household labour input.

As far as grain staples are concerned, the traditional form of cooking involved boiling them, in hulled but not polished form, in a stew with vegetables and other flavourings, using a pot suspended over a fire-pit. This relatively simple process did not involve exceptional amounts of labour or skill but keeping a hungry household labour force supplied with meals and snacks throughout the day depended on constant labour. In the region of Hida, for instance, up to World War II, the basic staple was barnyard millet, mixed with rice to varying degrees. It had to be milled every day using a water-driven mortar and was cooked and served in different mixes, depending on the status of the eater (Rath, 2016: 211). Such stews came to symbolise the poverty of rural life, even though meals based on mixed grains are more nutritious than those dominated by polished white rice that came to supersede them. As a result, in the cities and wherever incomes and commercial facilities permitted, one-pot stews were giving way, from the mid-Tokugawa period onwards, to the 'rice + side-dishes' meal pattern which characterised the samurai diet and continues to structure Japanese cuisine to this day. The key ingredient of such meals was polished white rice, steamed and served separately from a selection of side-dishes and pickles.

In the cities, most of the components of the rice + side-dishes meal could be acquired commercially from the shops, restaurants and street-sellers springing up to supply an urban population dominated by single men (Leupp, 1992: 29–41). For household-based caterers, however, serving rice in polished white form presented considerable challenges. Before the post-war invention of the electric rice-cooker, cooking the polished grain to create what we recognise as Japanese rice today was a skilled and time-consuming task, requiring attention and experience.

It could not be achieved through boiling over a fire-pit, but generally depended on the use of a stove, called a *kamado*, which incorporated separate cooking rings placed over fire-boxes in which fuel was burnt. These made it possible to control the heat at which the rice cooked over various stages, as well as enabling the cooking of several dishes at once. Such stoves, which were fitted items in kitchen areas, spread through the warmer areas of Japan wherever households had the space for them and the resources to acquire and operate them (Hanley, 1997: 63–64; Francks, 2009: 36–38). Rural households like those in Suye typically maintained their fire-pits for warmth and supplying hot water for tea, while constructing fitted *kamado* in separate kitchens (Embree, 1964: 91).

In many ways, use of the *kamado* improved the quality and variety of dishes that could be produced, even if the grain element in the meal was less nutritious. However, it also clearly increased the demands on cooks, in terms of time, knowledge and skill. Cooking white rice on a *kamado* requires considerable care and attention, if the rice is to achieve the desired consistency without burning, and it is necessary to raise and lower the temperature of the fire in the fire-box at various times during cooking to achieve the perfect result.[9] It opened up the possibilities for a more varied and tasty diet and Hanley (1997: 82) asserts that the growing popularity of the *kamado* 'attests to a rise in the standard of living and almost certainly a rise in the level of nutrition'. However, these improvements, and the labour and skill that went into them, cannot be reflected in standard estimates of GDP per capita, depending as they do on home-produced ingredients and the labour and management skills of an unpaid household labour force.

Meanwhile, from the later Tokugawa period onwards, urban households without the space or resources to accommodate a *kamado* were able to buy most of the elements of their meals from street-sellers and shops in forms such as pre-cooked rice, as well as sushi and ramen noodles. However portable charcoal grills called *shichirin* were also widespread and cheap to run, making grilled food a possibility, even in the small spaces in which many working families lived in the cities.[10] Tenement buildings

[9] Many electric rice-cookers now incorporate functions designed to recreate the 'authentic' taste of rice cooked on a *kamado*.

[10] The origin of the device's name is said to derive from the fact that the charcoal required to operate it cost seven (*shichi*) *rin* (a small Edo-period coin).

often provided communal facilities for washing and preparing ingredients and household labour could be mobilised for tasks such as fetching water and minding charcoal stoves. The grilled element in Japanese cuisine thus became established, partly as the speciality of street-sellers and restaurants, but also as a convenient way in which households could expand the range of their diets through their own labour.

The more complex meals made possible by improved kitchen facilities depended, not just on the preparation of grain, but also on the provision of the non-rice ingredients that supplied variety, nutrition and flavouring. Although fish in fresh or preserved forms became more widely available, as transport facilities improved, the main source of protein in the Japanese diet continued to be the soya bean. Farm households grew their own on upland fields or vegetable plots and then typically processed and preserved them in a number of forms. Chief among these was miso, the production of which involves boiling and mashing the beans before combining them with salt and a starter mix, which will bring on fermentation as the bean paste is stored and matured over months or years. Rural households for the most part possessed the equipment and storage space to produce their own miso, but even in the cities home-made miso seems to have been regarded as superior to 'shop-bought'. A middle-class housewife in 1910 Kyoto records in her diary how she bought in beans and organised the production of the household's miso at the appropriate time of year (Nakano, 1995: 213). The Suye villages were self-sufficient in it (Embree, 1964: Table 10), while, even in a poor family with limited resources, Partner's protagonist Toshié watched her mother make it (Partner, 2004: 20). Tofu is more tricky to make at home and does not keep like miso, so that eventually commercial suppliers became common even in villages (e.g. Embree, 1964: 53).

Miso is also commonly used as a flavouring ingredient, alongside the preserved fish and seaweed that became widely available through the Tokugawa period, but most flavourings and side-dishes were derived from vegetables and herbs, grown on garden plots or gathered in local woods and forests. Some such items were eaten fresh, but many were preserved to use as pickles or flavourings. This depended on household labour and knowledge and often the only purchased input required was salt, which was consumed in strikingly large amounts.[11] Vegetables were pickled for flavour as well as preservation, using salt, vinegar, rice-bran, sake lees, miso or other more specialised agents.[12]

Japanese supermarkets now display a bewildering range of these products, unrecognisable to the western consumer, which have their origins in the labour and skill of household workers. Most rural households were able to process daikon radish into the familiar yellow pickle (*takuan*) that accompanies typical Japanese meals; pickled plums (*umeboshi*) became ubiquitous accompaniments. Toshié's mother made *takuan* and *umeboshi*, as well as pickling a variety of other home-grown vegetables for use throughout the year (Partner, 2004: 20). In Hida in the 1930s, a pickle using red turnips became a local speciality, alongside a wide range based on other vegetables. Every meal or snack in a typical daily menu involved pickles, so that the organisation of pickling was deemed to be a key component of a Hida housewife's role in the household.[13]

Meals were always washed down with tea and, where appropriate, alcoholic drinks. In the Tokugawa period and into the Meiji, rural households continued to brew their own sake and stronger spirits (*shōchū*) distilled from grain or vegetables locally available (e.g. Rath, 2016: 214–215). They also found space to keep tea bushes and were able to grow and process their own tea (e.g. Embree, 1964: 43; see also Farris, 2019: 123–124). Both tea and sake were products that commercial producers were able to make to higher standards than small-scale households, and they expanded to supply the growing demand from households and entertainment facilities in the cities. Home-brewed sake remained common in rural areas, but the commercial product eventually came to dominate even there, as the retail network spread. Sake-brewing is no longer listed as a seasonal task in Suye in the 1930s (possibly because the government was trying to discourage home-brewing), although tea-picking and preparation still are (Embree, 1964: 51). Meanwhile commercial soy-sauce brewers were able to produce a product far superior to the substitute

---

[11] According to Gotō (2015: 94–95), average salt consumption per capita in late nineteenth-century Chōshū, for instance, was unhealthily high and might have contributed to the prevalence of various diseases.

[12] Hosking (1996: 145–146), dictionary entry under *tsukemono*.

[13] According to a local saying quoted by Rath, 'A mother who is bad at preparing miso and pickles is worse than a mother who can't sew' (Rath, 2016: 212).

that households could make and from relatively early on came to dominate the market in 'proper' soy-sauce. However, such reliance on the market for food was the exception rather than the rule outside the cities, so that the role of household labour in defining and producing the diet of industrialising Japan remained central.

CLOTHING

While food remained the largest item in the consumption basket of prewar Japanese households, clothing also took up a significant share. Like their counterparts elsewhere in the world, from time immemorial ordinary Japanese households had made their own clothing. Textile crops—principally flax and ramie—were grown on garden plots, processed and woven into the materials used for everyday clothing. The techniques of silk production had arrived in Japan from China and Korea in the early years AD but silk fabrics remained expensive luxury products, restricted as clothing materials to the samurai and aristocratic classes, until the second half of the Tokugawa period. The subsequent expansion in the market for silk was fuelled by the spread of commercial production in areas with suitable conditions, where filatures and workshops sprang up to process cocoons produced by rural households. By the later nineteenth century, Japanese silk had become a major export product but silk garments were still too expensive for most people, unless acquired second-hand, and most everyday clothing continued to be made up from home-produced linen and ramie.

What changed this, as in other parts of the world, was the spread of cotton production. Cotton-growing requires particular environmental conditions and came to be carried out in specialist regions as a commercial operation. Elsewhere, rural households came to engage with cotton production through contract employment in factories or within the home. On the consumption side within the household, meanwhile, cotton had a major impact, coming to replace home-grown yarns with a commercial product that resulted in more comfortable and practical clothing which could be dyed and woven into much more attractive colours and designs. Instead of the rather unrewarding labour of home-producing unexciting linen and ramie, women employed their textile skills on behalf of commercial producers who organised their work and the sale of their output, while purchasing cotton as yarn or cloth for their own use.

Nonetheless, although spinning and weaving of home-grown fibres began to die out, textile work for home use remained an important element in women's role within the household. Throughout the pre-World War II period, the vast majority of everyday Japanese clothing continued to take the form of kimono-type garments, accessorised with *obi* belts and various under- and over-garments. The kimono is in many ways a simple garment, made up from a bolt of cloth cut according to standard measurements and sewn together with straight seams. The interest in it lies in the design dyed or woven into the fabric and not in the sort of tailoring that determines fashion in Western-style clothing for men and women. Kimono-style garments were standardly taken apart for cleaning and the women of a household were expected to be able to do this and to sew the sections together again afterwards. This was a time-consuming, if not particularly difficult task, although the techniques used had to be adapted to the fabric of the garment and of course the neatness and accuracy that came with practice were valued and had to be learnt.[14] Meanwhile, kimono forms were adapted into working clothes, such as the *monpe* trousers that women were obliged to wear during the World War II period. Some rural women clearly continued to weave fabrics in traditional colours and patterns, as surviving examples in folklore collections attest (see Dalby, 2001: 172–176).

The significance attached to such activity reflected the fact that Japanese clothing materials represented long-lasting and relatively valuable assets for individuals and households. Girls worked to prepare trousseaux of clothing and bedding, which were expected to last a lifetime. They could be used as stores of wealth, pawned or sold when necessary, and they were typically the main item in dowries.[15] Their second-hand value was enhanced by their unfitted design which meant that they could easily be adapted to wearers of different shapes and sizes and they could be brought up-to-date with the use of accessories that reflected changing fashions (Francks, 2015). This depended on long-term care and maintenance on the part of the female household labour force.

---

[14] For a description of the sewing skills required of girls in late-Tokugawa households, see Stanley (2020: 15–17).

[15] When Stanley's protagonist Tsuneno ran away to Edo, her most pressing demand in letters to her family back in the country was that they should redeem the clothes she had pawned to fund her journey and sell the chest of items left behind and intended for her trousseau (e.g. Stanley, 2020: 94–95).

The skills involved in mending and patching came to be highly appreciated and their influence on the look of Japanese textiles has persisted to this day. The embroidery technique known as *sashiko*, for example, developed as the means to secure patches and in due course to strengthen fabric all over, gave rise to the indigo and white, straight-line geometric patterns still common in Japanese textile design.

The infrastructure of knowledge, skills and practices that sustained the work of maintaining and caring for clothing on the part of household workers survived and adapted through to the post-World War II period. This was despite the introduction of Western-style clothing, which remained largely limited to the fashionable in the cities and to particular practical uses, such as in military and other uniforms. In other parts of the world, the inter-war period saw the spread of the sewing machine, which enabled both households and commercial businesses to produce relatively complex clothing styles for themselves. However, in Japan, the sewing machine was deemed unsuited to sewing kimono seams—and indeed unpicking the tight stitching produced by a machine for regular washing purposes would have been challenging—so that it was only with the full-scale switch to Western-style clothing after the war that Japanese women and girls invested in machines and poured into sewing schools to learn how to use them (Gordon, 2012: ch7).

Hence, for most women, the purpose of buying a sewing machine and learning to use it was so as to be able to make Western-style clothes for their families at home. Although men's Western-style clothes were increasingly produced by commercial tailors, mass-produced clothes for women and children remained in relatively limited demand,[16] so that the switch to Western-style clothing of the post-war decades was largely achieved through the labour of household workers. This required the learning of new skills, hence the popularity of sewing schools, but it resulted in the mobilisation of the female household labour force as 'a nation of dressmakers, seamstresses, and home-sewing housewives' (Gordon, 2012: 196). How much of the output of such activity ever made it into GDP statistics cannot be known, but it seems not unreasonable to suppose that unpaid household workers continued, as in the pre-war period, to make a substantial unrecorded contribution to

[16] Around 1960, 95% of women's clothing in the United States was bought ready-made, compared with 40% in Japan (Gordon, 2012: 196).

the improving living standards of Japanese households through the production and maintenance of clothing.

By the 1970s, as more and more women entered the employed labour force and international trade made globalised mass-produced fashion cheap and available, Japanese consumers finally turned to commercial suppliers for their clothing, but until then home-sewing remained a skill that even the modern housewife needed to command. Throughout Japan's industrial development, therefore, the labour involved in producing and maintaining clothing, as everyday wear and as a valuable asset, made an unmeasurable contribution to output and its growth, as well as imposing lasting patterns on the nature of everyday consumer goods.

OTHER GOODS AND SERVICES

Up to World War II, despite the introduction of Western-style infrastructure—trains, electricity, telephone systems, etc.—the living environment of most Japanese households remained governed by 'traditional' styles. The general construction and maintenance of the houses in which they lived depended on specialists from outside the household, in particular the carpenters who built and maintained the wooden structures of most buildings and the tatami makers who covered the floors. With rising incomes and the increasing availability of cotton during the Tokugawa period, the use of proper bedding spread, in the form of futons, which were typically sewn by women to include in their trousseaux (Hanley, 1997: 48). Otherwise, Japanese houses remained sparsely furnished and the beds, wardrobes and dining tables that European households began to acquire as reflections of rising income and status were substituted by limited amounts of fixtures and fittings, mainly for storage of bedding and clothing.[17] The cleaning and polishing that cluttered Western-style interiors imposed on the work-time of family members and servants in Europe and North America did not perhaps represent the same burden for their Japanese counterparts.

Other, often overlooked, activities were however essential to the lives and comfort of Japanese households. The main source of fuel for heating

---

[17] The more fashionable in the cities maintained Western-style rooms within their otherwise Japanese-style houses, filling them with furniture and objects that no doubt needed to be dusted. See Sand (2003: 105–107).

and cooking remained charcoal—the most efficient form in which to make use of the wood that was the only abundant fuel-source under Japanese conditions until the arrival of gas and electricity supplies to the cities after 1900. Commercial charcoal-makers seem to have been common by the Tokugawa period, but rural households, at least, continued to make it for themselves during the winter months (Hanley, 1997: 62–63). Farm households in Suye were still acquiring almost all their charcoal and firewood in kind in the inter-war period, although it was by then mainly produced by workers in the upland hamlet of the village as a commercial enterprise (Embree, 1964: 318–319). Outside the cities, water had to be drawn and fetched from wells; child-minding was an important activity, typically allocated to older children and grandparents, given that the adult female members of the household were often fully occupied with agriculture and side-employments and school attendance was sporadic until the late nineteenth century.

In such ways, the whole household could be mobilised in a range of activities that supported their living standards and generated income, some of which might be paid and others not. Such a mobilisation required management and this was generally assumed to be the responsibility of the house-head's wife. In commercial enterprises in particular, the wife of the head typically kept the accounts, and an understanding of business finance was something else required of incoming brides.[18] Buying and selling, pawnbroking, brothel-keeping—there is a lengthy list of occupations that women undertook while remaining members of households, some formally paid but many generating unrecorded income subsumed into the household pot.

Finally, it is worth noting that life in pre-industrial and industrialising Japan was not necessarily all work. Every village and urban neighbourhood had its own seasonal round of festivals and ceremonies; troupes of actors and musicians travelled round the countryside; weddings, births, roof topping-outs, the completion of transplanting and harvesting and much else offered opportunities for communal celebration. Such events almost always involved banquets which of course depended on the unpaid labour of local women to supply and serve the food and drink. Eventually the range of commercial entertainment—the cinema, radio, travel

---

[18] See the nice example of a Tokugawa-period writing school in Rubinger (2007: 124). 'Wifely business acumen and facility with accounts was not seen as warranting anything more than passing reference in records of nineteenth-century merchant families'.

and sightseeing—began to expand, even for those in the countryside, and commercial catering services became more common. But the role of unpaid and unrecorded household labour in supporting the life of the community and its enjoyment should not be forgotten. The survival of the strong village community which has characterised rural Japanese society since the Tokugawa period owes much to the unpaid catering activities of village women.

The Japanese Consumption Pattern and the Role of Women

The previous sections can therefore be taken to suggest that, by the second half of the Tokugawa period, a distinctive consumption pattern was becoming established across Japan, as the productivity of land and labour resources rose, enabling households to improve and diversify their living standards. Certainly, consumption goods remained constrained by 'traditional' forms and largely immune to outside influences, but this did not mean that they were unchanging. Given the ways in which they were produced, such change was by no means labour-saving, so that increases in output placed new demands on household labour forces. However, making the link between increased labour input and the actual content of work performed—hence the possible relationship between rising living standards and unpaid household labour—is problematic, in the absence of the kind of time-use data used today to reveal the distribution of work tasks.

Qualitative accounts do of course provide snippets of information about work organisation within the household in the nineteenth and early twentieth centuries. They typically show the household head's wife as bearing the brunt of household labour and its organisation, but any other older women in the labour force were also expected to contribute to agricultural activities and side-line work such as silk-cocoon production. Heavy agricultural work was necessarily men's responsibility but as crop yields increased, the labour demands of cultivation activity typically assigned to women, such as transplanting and harvesting, not to mention the processing of crops for sale or home consumption, would have risen in line. Men do seem to have helped out with the heavier work, while grandparents and children could be mobilised for tasks such as child-minding. Nonetheless, the range of paid and unpaid productive activities assigned to women within urban and rural households appears to have been large and growing, as production expanded from the later Tokugawa period onwards (see e.g. Uno, 1991: 26–30, 33–34).

For a later period, however, the inter-war Farm Household Economy surveys do record some time-use data, enabling Tanimoto to analyse the distribution of work in farming households in a more systematic way, even if the sample numbers are small and not necessarily totally representative (Tanimoto, 2012). These data confirm that male household members on average devoted themselves largely to cultivation and other income-earning activities, as did the house-head's wife, while older and younger women provided the majority of the housework hours. It seems there was no strict division of labour between male and female workers as regards income-earning work, but housework was predominantly performed by a combination of the female household members. Housework hours were dominated by cooking, which accounted for an average of 6 hours work per day (Tanimoto, 2012: 33), followed at some distance by childcare and sewing. Relatively little time seems to have been spent on cleaning and washing.

This suggests that housework was predominantly a matter of producing goods for consumption by the household—mainly food and clothing—and Tanimoto (2012: 37–41) is able to show that housework hours in the surveys correlate most strongly, on the demand side, with household expenditure (in cash and kind), and on the supply side with the number of female household members available. That is to say, as the consumption of goods rises, so does the demand for housework, implying that, in the context of the Japanese consumption pattern and the nature of the goods involved, a complementary relationship existed between living standards and the unpaid labour of female household members.

Equivalent data to the FHE do not exist for urban households but Tanimoto is able to use what information is available to suggest that the pattern of labour use within the household followed that in rural households, especially within the small-scale businesses that dominated the pre-war urban-industrial sector in cities such as Tokyo and Osaka. Housework was managed by the house-head's wife who also often assisted her husband in the business as well (Tanimoto, 2012: 9). However urban households typically contained fewer female relatives than rural ones, so that maintenance of desired living standards, given the labour demands of the consumption pattern, might depend on the ability to hire a domestic servant. Employment in domestic service did expand rapidly in the inter-war period, coming to represent the largest occupation of employed women (Tanimoto, 2012: 45). Hence a smaller share of the housework may have been performed by unpaid family workers, but the management requirements demanded of the house-head's wife must have increased. The emerging model of the 'good wife, wise mother', increasingly promoted in the media and by the state, was thus as a manager of the supply of consumer goods, even if an increasing share of these involved 'modern' elements that could only be acquired in the market.

For women in poorer urban households, as Uno (1993) describes, piecework in the home often provided an essential supplement to household income but clearly interfered with the ability to perform household tasks. In the early stages of industrial urbanisation from the late nineteenth century onwards, incoming households in the cities typically lived in one-room apartments with shared facilities, lacking the space or equipment, as well as the time, for individual cooking. However, by the inter-war period, incomes had risen and many were able to rent apartments with private cooking areas. Whereas they had previously relied on pre-cooked dishes bought from street-sellers and local shops, female household members were now expected to take on the demanding tasks involved in producing Japanese-style meals for the family—lighting and minding the stove, fetching water, preparing vegetables and so on—and most were by then eating white rice rather than grain mixes (Uno, 1991: 55–56). Hence, among the urban poorer classes too, increases in living standards and the achievement of a 'respectable' lifestyle depended on the unpaid labour of female household members, even if fitted in alongside paid work or self-employment.

Through the pre-World-War II period, therefore, as long as small-scale cultivation and widespread self-sufficiency prevailed, rising living standards, and indeed the 'modernisation' of Japanese diets and lifestyles in both rural and urban environments, would depend on the mobilisation of household labour. Dietary change and improvements to cooking methods were not for the most part labour-saving in Japan before the post-war period, so that the demands on housewife-managers only increased, as the elements of Japanese cuisine in the form we now know became available to a widening range of consumers. This was the case among the expanding number of urban households, as well as rural ones, given the nature of the products that continued to constitute the everyday diet. Meanwhile, the supply of clothing continued to depend on home-sewing time and skills for its maintenance. As a result, housewifely skills remained central to the definition of women's role within the household, whether the inspiration was 'traditional' or 'modern'. In its advice and propaganda, the state reinforced this process, increasingly promoting the 'good wife, wise mother' (*ryōsei kenbo*) as the model of women's role in economy and society.

By the post-war period, as urbanisation and industrialisation boomed, more and more women, alongside their husbands, brothers and fathers, came to engage in paid employment and to rely on commercially supplied goods and services to support their household's rising living standards. As a result, as Gordon puts it, the role of the housewife switched from that of producer to that of purchasing manager (Gordon, 2012: 213). However, the influence of the past abundance of unpaid household labour on the consumption pattern remained, as the Japanese diet continued to be dominated by the labour-intensively produced goods—rice, miso, pickles and so on—that households had devised and manufactured, even if these were now factory-made. Tastes and designs made possible through the time and skill of household workers still permeate the consumption pattern and characterise many of the Japanese products that appeal to global consumers.

Meanwhile, the role of women in the household and the labour force in Japan has continued to be conditioned by the long history of unpaid household activities that women performed. The indispensability of female workers within the household labour force meant that their participation in employment outside the home was restricted to limited periods at particular stages in their lives and this continues to be reflected in the institutions and attitudes governing female labour force participation. Politicians contemplating Japan's dwindling native-born population may rail against the failure of Japanese women to 'do their duty' but it is difficult to avoid the conclusion that the burdens of producing the Japanese consumption pattern on a daily basis might well have played a part in making marriage and motherhood unattractive to young women in the modern world.

It has to be concluded, therefore, that the value added by the labour devoted to maintaining and improving the household's living standard under Japanese conditions is surely significant, even if impossible to measure. Of course, everywhere in the world, crops have to be processed into consumable items, but who does this processing and hence whether or not its value is included in measures such as GDP depends on the wide range of technological, institutional and economic factors described earlier. The characteristics of the Japanese diet suggest that the availability of household labour offered widespread scope for the production of items that required significant inputs of time, skill and knowledge on the part of household members, chiefly the female ones. In many ways, it is these products, even if nowadays often adapted to factory production, that characterise the Japanese cuisine that has spread around the world and the domestic consumption pattern that conditions the everyday life of Japanese households.

REFERENCES

Ågren, M. (2018). The complexities of work: Analyzing men's and women's work in the early modern world with the verb-oriented method. In R. Sarti, A. Bellavitis, & M. Martini (Eds.), *What is work? Gender at the crossroads of home, family, and business from the early modern era to the present*. Berghahn Books.

Bassino, J.-P., Broadberry, S., Fukao, K., Gupta, B., & Takashima, M. (2019). Japan and the great divergence, 730–1874. *Explorations in Economic History, 72*, 1–22.

Bernstein, G. (2005). *Isami's house: Three centuries of a Japanese family*. University of California Press.

Collins, E. J. T. (1993). Why wheat? Choice of food grains in Europe in the nineteenth and twentieth centuries. *Journal of European Economic History, 22*(1), 7–38.

Dalby, L. (2001). *Kimono: Fashioning culture*. Vintage.

Embree, J. (1964). *Suye Mura: A Japanese village* (Rev. ed.). University of Chicago Press.

Farris, W. (2019). *A bowl for a coin: A commodity history of Japanese tea*. University of Hawai'i Press.

Francks, P. (2006). *Rural economic development in Japan: from the nineteenth century to the Pacific War*. Routledge.

Francks, P. (2009). *The Japanese consumer; an alternative economic history of modern Japan*. Cambridge University Press.

Francks, P. (2015). Was fashion a European invention? The kimono and economic development in Japan. *Fashion Theory, 19*(3), 331–361. https://doi.org/10.2752/175174115X14223685749368

Francks, P. (2021). Industriousness and divergence: Living standards, housework and the Japanese diet in comparative historical perspective. *Australian Economic History Review, 1–21*. https://doi.org/10.1111/aehr.122222021

Gordon, A. (2012). *Fabricating consumers: The sewing machine in modern Japan*. University of California Press.

Gotō, Y. (2015). *Edo no Shoku ni Manabu: Bakumatsu Chōshū-han no Eiyō Jijō* (Studying the Edo diet: Nutrition in late-Tokugawa Chōshū). Rinsen Shoten.

Hanley, S. (1997). *Everyday things in premodern Japan*. University of California Press.

Hosking, R. (1996). *A dictionary of Japanese food: Ingredients and culture*. Tuttle.

Leupp, G. P. (1992). *Servants, shophands, and laborers in the cities of Tokugawa Japan*. Princeton University Press.

Nakano, M. (1995). *Makiko's diary: A merchant wife in 1910 Kyoto* (K. Smith, Trans.). Stanford University Press.

Partner, S. (2004). *Toshié: A story of village life in twentieth-century Japan*. University of California Press.

Rath, E. (2016) *Japan's cuisines: Food, place and identity*. Reaktion Books, Kindle edition.

Rubinger, R. (2007). *Popular literacy in early modern Japan*. University of Hawai'i Press.

Sand, J. (2003). *House and home in modern Japan: Architecture, domestic space, and bourgeois culture, 1880–1930*. Harvard University Press.

Shepard, A. (2015). Crediting women in the early modern English economy. *History Workshop Journal, 79*, 1–24.

Smith, T. (1959). *The agrarian origins of modern Japan*. Stanford University Press.

Stanley, A. (2020). *Stranger in the Shogun's city: A woman's life in nineteenth-century Japan*. Chatto & Windus.

Tanimoto, M. (2012). The role of housework in everyday life; another aspect of consumption in modern Japan. In P. Francks & J. Hunter (Eds.), *The historical consumer: Consumption and everyday life in Japan, 1850–2000* (pp. 27–55). Palgrave Macmillan.

Taueber, I. (1958). *The population of Japan*. Princeton University Press.

Uno, K. (1991). Women and changes in the household division of labor. In G. Bernstein (Ed.), *Recreating Japanese women, 1600–1945* (pp. 17–41). University of California Press.

Uno, K. (1993). One day at a time: Work and domestic activities of urban lower-class women in early twentieth-century Japan. In J. Hunter (Ed.), *Japanese women working* (pp. 37–68). Routledge.

Yamakawa, K. (2001). *Women of the Mito domain: Recollections of Samurai family life* (K. W. Nakai, Trans.). Stanford University Press.

CHAPTER 5

Conclusion

Abstract This brief chapter draws together the arguments made in the book. Up to the inter-war period at least, the Japanese economy was characterised by small-scale production units and a high level of household self-sufficiency, especially in food. This depended on the availability of household labour, which was unpaid according to the 'third-party criterion' and not reflected in standard quantitative measures of living standards. Examination of the characteristics of the diet and clothing consumed by rural and urban households reveals the role of such labour in determining living standards and the significance of its neglect in historical assessments and comparisons. It also highlights the influence of female household labour in the creation of food products that have come to be enjoyed across the globe in recent years.

Keywords Comparative historical living standards · Unpaid household labour · Women's work in Japan · Origins of Japanese food products

This book has sought to argue that the neglect of unpaid household labour and its contribution to production and living standards distorts our understanding of the comparative history of economic growth and industrialisation across the globe. Chapter 2 summarises the growing

© The Author(s), under exclusive license to Springer Nature   69
Switzerland AG 2025
P. Francks, *Housework, Consumption and Female Labour in Japan,*
1600–1940, Palgrave Studies in Economic History,
https://doi.org/10.1007/978-3-031-83693-0_5

body of literature demonstrating, mainly for England and other parts of Europe, the significant and varied role played by household-based workers, predominantly women, in pre-industrial and industrialising societies. The evidence suggests that this role encompassed much more than the 'housework and childcare' assigned to women in the standard estimates of GDP per capita and used to justify assumptions of a limited and unvarying contribution by household and female workers. The much broader scope of the 'third-party' definition of 'unpaid' productive activities makes it possible to take account, at least qualitatively, of the many forms of work that empirical studies observe household workers fitting round their housework and caring obligations.

Unpaid labour therefore matters because it helps to sustain and improve living standards and because it can be a major way in which women take part in economic activity. However, it is very hard to observe and assess. This book attempts to approach the issues involved through a case study of Japan during its period of growth and industrialisation from the later eighteenth century to World War II, thereby also broadening the possibilities of comparison beyond the European examples which have so far dominated the literature. Chapter 3 summarises the broad economic and institutional structures which could be taken to determine the scope for unpaid household labour and which can, to some extent, be compared across national and cultural boundaries. Japan remained a society of small-scale businesses, many with access to land which could be used to grow crops for household consumption. It can be hypothesised that the resulting high rate of household self-sufficiency, especially in food, must have generated substantial amounts of unrecorded and unpaid work for household members and a significant, but unmeasurable, contribution to economic output.

The institutional and family structures that supported small-scale business and agriculture throughout the period operated to ensure the supply of labour to meet the necessary work requirements. The three-generational *ie* structure provided a framework for adjusting household labour supply to work demands, mainly by means of flexible roles for women. Evidence suggests that female workers were increasingly valued, within agricultural and small-business households, but that wage-work outside the household continued to be regarded as no more than a short-term stage in their working lives. Micro histories give us examples: Toshié and her mother (Partner, 2004), for instance, worked hard at household tasks which would certainly meet the third-party test but for which they do not appear to have received any individual payment. However, wider evidence of the nature of unpaid labour and its contribution to output is difficult to find.

Chapter 4 therefore tries to tackle this problem from a different angle. It argues that the nature of the Japanese consumption pattern and the goods in which it is embodied imply a gap between measurable output and the value of the goods constituting final consumption that might well be larger than in those societies where reliance on market-supplied goods was greater. This gap was filled by the output of unpaid household labour, much of it female, and took the form of labour-intensively produced food and other consumption goods. As a result, Japanese cuisine to this day is embodied in products such as carefully steamed rice, pickles and miso that mothers and daughters once laboured to produce unpaid within their households.

This has two major implications. Firstly, it implies that, in Japan as in other industrialising countries, if we could take account of the contribution of unpaid household labour to overall output, pre-industrial production and living standards would be seen to be higher than estimates based on measurable inputs and output suggest. As now appears to have been the case for, say, England, the process that culminated in industrialisation involved a longer and slower process than the dramatic 'Industrial Revolution' model implies.[1] The diet and clothing available to pre-industrial consumers, embodying as they did the results of intensive and often skilled household labour, could have been more abundant, varied and high-quality than statistical measures of output imply, suggesting a higher-level starting-point and a more gradual progression towards the conditions for industrialisation.

This would be especially the case where households continued to have available to them, as a result of their own self-subsistent labour, the inputs that formed the basis of the consumption pattern. In the Japanese case, relatively secure rights to landholdings have made historically high levels of self-sufficiency possible, generating the raw materials that household labour could transform into the elements of the now globally enjoyed Japanese diet. Chapter 3 argues that the institutional and technological conditions that underpinned the prevalence of small-scale cultivation and high levels of household self-sufficiency were emerging in Tokugawa

---

[1] For a survey of the English case, see Griffen (2010: ch 2).

Japan, leading to a distinctive consumption pattern and a crucial role for unpaid household labour in general, and women's work in particular. The significance of women's unpaid contribution to household welfare and survival was increasingly reflected both in the characteristics of consumer products and in the value attached to women's role in the household, and this has continued to condition the nature of women's participation in the labour force ever since.

The second implication involves the comparative consequences of the relative under-measurement of final output under Japanese conditions. Evidence that the under-estimation of pre-industrial levels of output per capita and living standards was greater in Japan than in other examples of industrialisation, as a result of the greater role of unpaid household labour, strengthens Pomeranz's argument that differences in pre-industrial economic and social conditions were not sufficient to explain why industrialisation took off in northern Europe and not in East Asia. Within an institutional structure predicated on small-scale production and the flexible deployment of household labour time, pre-industrial Japan was able to generate economic growth, the diffusion of improved technology, investment in infrastructure and communications, and the development of the skills and knowledge that would in due course make possible the establishment of modern industry.

Hence, if it is the case that unpaid household labour played a more significant and long-lasting role in Japanese economic development than it did in other industrialising nations, the implications of this need to be explored if we are to understand global patterns of economic development through history. There is probably nothing that can be done to improve the measurability of the household labour contribution to the Japanese economy, but the literature on Europe suggests there may be ingenious sources of evidence as to women's work (and non-work) activities in the past. A range of micro-level case studies is emerging, detailing the lives of individual women and families, which can be mined for descriptive accounts of household work and its distribution. However, recognition of the significance of household labour, and differences in its historic role in economic development across the globe, might encourage more focused attempts to raise women's work from obscurity. After all, the results of the long history of household labour in Japan are now available to all of us in shops and restaurants across the world—just another element in the unrecognised significance of unpaid women's work to the economic world in which we now live.

REFERENCES

Griffen, E. (2010). *A short history of the British industrial revolution.* Palgrave Macmillan.

Partner, S. (2004). *Toshié: A story of village life in twentieth-century Japan.* University of California Press.

INDEX

The manufacturer's authorised representative in the EU is Springer
Nature Customer Service Centre GmbH, Europaplatz 3, 69115 Heidelberg,
Germany. If you have any concerns regarding our products, please
contact ProductSafety@springernature.com

Printed and bound by CPI Group (UK) Ltd, Croydon, CR0 4YY
29/04/2026
02099545-0002